# Praise for the First Edition

"A timely and provocative book concerning Christian resources of faith in a culture besot by fear. Bader-Saye's diagnosis of a pervasive system of anxiety, rooted in Enlightenment reductionism, is on target; but more important is his assessment of the capacity of communitarian courage to act as a transformative alternative to fear. Bader-Saye draws upon compelling contemporary cases of such courageous action but shows, with equally compelling articulation, how such courage finally is deeply rooted in God's providence."
—**Walter Brueggemann**, Columbia Theological Seminary

"[A] cogently argued and elegantly written volume."
—*Publishers Weekly*

"A call to discipleship in its truest form—without obsession and preoccupation with the costs or dangers of daily life. . . . Once we begin to understand that God is present with us in whatever circumstances surround our lives, ultimately redeeming every event of human existence, fear can be put in its place."
—**Kathy Brawley**, *Covenant Companion*

"Offers us Christian practical wisdom we desperately need. Through insightful examples as well as rich biblical and theological analysis, Bader-Saye beautifully invites us to trust God and to risk hospitality, peacemaking, and generosity. A profoundly hopeful, and hope-filled, book."
—**L. Gregory Jones**, Duke Divinity School

"A timely and well-written book."
—**Anthony B. Robinson**, *The Christian Century*

"The book is challenging and encouraging, and the discussion questions at the end of each chapter make it an ideal small-group resource."
—**Derek Melleby**, *Engage*

"Bader-Saye shares a great perspective on fear, one of the most abused commodities in our culture. His encouragement to follow Jesus is exactly the antidote we need."
—**John Dunham**, *YouthWorker Journal*

"Through helpful use of movie scenes and popular novels, and serious Bible study, Scott helps us all move towards a life of love, learning to embody the hospitality of Christ, and engage in peacemaking ministries. Good discussion questions, too, making this an ideal tool for study groups."
—B

T0385861

# Other books by the author

*Formed by Love*

*Church and Israel after Christendom: The Politics of Election*

Revised and Updated Edition

# FOLLOWING JESUS IN A CULTURE OF FEAR

Choosing Trust over Safety in an Anxious Age

## SCOTT BADER-SAYE

BrazosPress

*a division of Baker Publishing Group*
Grand Rapids, Michigan

© 2007, 2020 by Scott Bader-Saye

Published by Brazos Press
a division of Baker Publishing Group
PO Box 6287, Grand Rapids, MI 49516-6287
www.brazospress.com

Previous edition published in 2007

Printed in the United States of America

Library of Congress Cataloging-in-Publication Data
Names: Bader-Saye, Scott, author.
Title: Following Jesus in a culture of fear : choosing trust over safety in an anxious age / Scott Bader-Saye.
Description: Revised and updated edition. | Grand Rapids, Michigan : Brazos Press, a division of Baker Publishing Group, 2020.
Identifiers: LCCN 2020018563 | ISBN 9781587434525 (paperback) | ISBN 9781587435157 (casebound)
Subjects: LCSH: Fear—Religious aspects—Christianity. | Christianity and culture. | Providence and government of God—Christianity. | Christian life.
Classification: LCC BV4908.5 .B33 2020 | DDC 248.4—dc23
LC record available at https://lccn.loc.gov/2020018563

20  21  22  23  24  25  26      7  6  5  4  3  2  1

In keeping with biblical principles of creation stewardship, Baker Publishing Group advocates the responsible use of our natural resources. As a member of the Green Press Initiative, our company uses recycled paper when possible. The text paper of this book is composed in part of post-consumer waste.

To Demery
Who taught my heart not to fear
and whose presence in my life
is a sure sign of God's providence

Most loving Father, whose will it is for us to give thanks for all things, to fear nothing but the loss of you, and to cast all our care on you who care for us: Preserve us from faithless fears and worldly anxieties, that no clouds of this mortal life may hide from us the light of that love which is immortal, and which you have manifested to us in your Son Jesus Christ our Lord; who lives and reigns with you, in the unity of the Holy Spirit, one God, now and for ever. *Amen.*

—Collect for the Eighth Sunday after Epiphany
*The Book of Common Prayer*

My thesis . . . is very simply stated, though it has two parts: first, contemporary America is full of fear. And second, fear is not a Christian habit of mind.

—Marilynne Robinson

# CONTENTS

# ACKNOWLEDGMENTS

Thanks to the many people and institutions who helped make this book possible. First, thanks to the Louisville Institute, whose Christian Faith and Life Sabbatical Grant provided significant time and funding for research and conversation. Thanks also to the Institute staff and my fellow grantees who provided helpful feedback on early drafts of these ideas. I am grateful to the Passionist Nuns of St. Gabriel's Retreat Center in Clarks Summit, Pennsylvania, for providing a peaceful space to work on the first edition during my sabbatical. Thanks to those who read and commented on drafts of chapters: Raymond Barfield, Pauline Palko, Mary Reed, Dan Shenk-Evans, Alice Townley, and Allison Treat. Your insights and suggestions helped make the final draft clearer and more accessible. I owe a debt to those who allowed me to use their personal stories as examples of living honestly and well in a culture of fear: Kate Brennan, Maureen Fiordimondo, Ollie and Heather Wagner, Bob Fox, and David Daily. Your lives of faith are an encouragement to me. Thanks to my editors at Brazos Press—Rodney Clapp, Rebecca Cooper, Katelyn Beaty, and Eric Salo—whose suggestions and support made this a better book. Thanks to the *Journal of the Society of Christian Ethics* for permission to reprint portions of "Thomas Aquinas and the Culture of Fear" in volume 25, no. 2 (2005), 95–108, in chapter 4. Thanks to Wipf and Stock and *Ex Auditu* for permission to reprint portions of "Fear in the Garden: The State of Emergency and the Politics of Blessing," *Ex Auditu* 24 (2008): 1–13, in chapter 7.

My biggest thanks go to my family—to Elise, Eli, and Luke, who bring me joy and give me eyes to see, and to my wife, Demery, whose unflagging support kept me writing and whose superb editorial skill contributed to the text in countless ways.

# PREFACE

I remember being thirteen years old and, as a requirement for confirmation class, having to memorize the Twenty-Third Psalm. I was in eighth grade, and in addition to taking confirmation class I was making my way through *The Lord of the Rings* for the first time. So, every Sunday evening, as my parents drove me to the church, I would be reading Tolkien in the back seat.

The thematic confluence between these two activities occurred when the journey of Frodo and Samwise through the dark paths of Mordor met the refrain of the psalmist, "Yea, though I walk through the valley of the shadow of death, I will fear no evil: for thou art with me" (Ps. 23:4 KJV). My aspirational teenage heart wanted to be heroic like Frodo and Sam, yet it knew that any real-life version of the journey to destroy the ring of power could easily become a road map to failure and hurt. In that space of teenage aspiration and fear, the words of the psalmist spoke to my anxieties, and they have stayed with me like a companion ever since. If Frodo and Sam could be sustained by courage, friendship, a bit of magic, and the background machinations of Gandalf, then surely I could be sustained by friendship with the God who is "with me."

Perhaps no other biblical verse can claim as much cultural ubiquity as Psalm 23:4. But it misses, perhaps, one aspect of fear—that fear is not only what we feel when passing through the valley of the shadow of death; it is one of the *causes* of the valley of the shadow of death. Pope Francis succinctly summarizes this deadly power of fear:

> Fear . . . is fed, manipulated. . . . Because fear is . . . good business for those who trade in weapons and death, it weakens us, throws us off balance, breaks down our psychological and spiritual defenses, anaesthetizes us to the sufferings of others, and in the end makes us cruel. When we . . . see that war is preferred to peace, when we see the spread of xenophobia, when we realize that intolerant ideas are gaining ground, behind that burgeoning cruelty is the cold breath of fear.[1]

This cold breath of fear, this "valley of the shadow of death," makes itself known in various ways in our lives. My valley is inhabited by a low underbrush of anxiety about the well-being of my family, especially as I imagine the future for my children; it is populated by vines of trepidation for friends and acquaintances who by virtue of their race, religion, immigration status, sexual orientation, or gender identity face threats that they should not have to face; my valley of the shadow of death is overarched by trees whose limbs twist and turn with the menace of global threats—climate change, warfare, water crises, disease, and poverty; and snaking through my valley is a disorienting and disempowering mist that makes it hard to find my next steps.

Twelve years have passed since the first edition of this book was published, and the culture of fear is as pervasive as ever. The chief objects of fear have shifted, though some perennial fears simply take on new forms over time. As I write this, a global pandemic has struck much of the world, creating fear of contagion and death as well as worry about the consequences of economic shutdown. The trauma of September 11 has waned over two decades, but Muslims and Arab nations remain, for some, sources of anxiety. Much of the political fear in the US and Europe focuses on immigration, national identity, and economic globalization. The fears of some about immigrants are met by the fears of others about nationalism. Climate change anxiety deepens as we watch sea levels rise and experience extreme weather patterns. Some parents continue to worry about vaccinations, while others worry that unvaccinated children will bring a recurrence of diseases we thought were behind us. Every December, conspiracy theorists raise alarms about a "war on Christmas."

As president, Donald Trump has proven to be a master manipulator of fear. In fact, he admits that stoking fear is part of his political strategy. "Real power is—I don't even want to use the word—fear," he told Bob Woodward and Robert Costa in an interview.[2] He was, knowingly or not, echoing Machiavelli's advice to rulers that it is better to be feared than loved. But Trump's audacious and unscrupulous manipulation of fear makes Machiavelli look moderate.

As I edited this revised edition, I paid attention to the fact that my audience does not consist only of those whose status yields the safety necessary to worry about being too afraid. Since this book first came out, I have spoken to faith communities, civic groups, and universities on the topic of fear and faith. In doing so, I became aware that my talks were assuming an audience of people like me—those whose lives were relatively safe but who could be caught up in manufactured or excessive fear that would lead us from the good God intends for us. I wasn't aware of how the talks might be heard by a different audience until I was speaking to a group of Muslims at an Islamic Center near Toronto. As I moved into my presentation, I sensed that the talk was missing its mark, that this audience needed to hear something different. They were not in a relatively safe place where they needed to be aware of false fears; they were actually in a precarious place because they were the feared ones whose lives had become less secure. The perspective of the scapegoat and the marginalized was on my mind as I reworked this text.

Both the fearful and the feared share the threat of being overwhelmed by the cultural anxiety that constricts our lives, threatens our solidarity, and makes us less than we could be. "There are always real dangers in the world, sufficient to their day," the novelist Marilynne Robinson reminds us. "Fearfulness obscures the distinction between real threat on one hand and on the other the terrors that beset those who see threat everywhere."[3] This book is an attempt to help us parse this distinction. It is also, and perhaps most importantly, a book about hope. But to get to hope we have to pass through fear. We can't avoid it or deny it. And we have to understand where fear comes from if we are going to resist its control.

# Fear for Profit

*Do not be afraid.* We live in a time when this biblical refrain cannot be repeated too often. Among all the things the church has to say today, this may be the most important. No one has to be convinced that we live in fearful times, though we are not always sure what we should be afraid of and why. We suspect that our fears make us vulnerable to manipulation, but we find it hard to quell the fear long enough to analyze how it is being produced and directed for the benefit of others.

Using fear to gain power, make money, or win converts has a long pedigree. The object of fear almost seems an afterthought. The key move is to exaggerate a real threat or construct an artificial threat that can then siphon people's energy, money, and loyalty toward a person, product, or cause that can make us feel safe again. The "again" is important since the most effective fearmongering conjures nostalgia for an imaginary time when "we" were all safe. For this to work, the threat has to be minimal though not nonexistent, since there needs to be a spark of fear to be fanned. The object of fear is often a threatening other, and all that is needed to ignite the spark is one high-profile event that causes harm or destruction. For instance, in the United States, leaders have stoked unreasonable levels of fear toward Latinx immigrants, Muslims, Black men, and, in generations past, communists, Irish, Italians, Germans, Catholics, Jews, and Mormons. Sometimes the exaggerated fear is not directed at people but cultural or technological advances (remember when your cell phone was going to give you cancer if you held it too close to your ear or kept it in your pants pocket?).

In each case, fear is either misdirected or exaggerated for the sake of someone who will profit from the perception of insecurity. But what if the path out of fear is not through power but trust, not through strength but vulnerability? What if a risk-free life can only be purchased by trading our best aspirations for our basest inclinations?

## Fearful Parenting

My wife and I experienced a new level of fear when we had our first child. Eager to master this new challenge, we took to the books soon after learning Demery was pregnant. From *What to Expect When You're Expecting* to *Husband-Coached Childbirth*, we investigated what the experts were saying. We quickly realized we were in territory littered with land mines. From pregnancy to parenting, we wanted to do the right thing in a situation where it was no longer self-evident what the "right thing" was. Should we have the baby at home with a midwife? Should we hire a doula to assist my wife and attend to her comfort? Should we take advantage of the full medical and technological capacities of the modern hospital, trusting ourselves to well-trained doctors and nurses? If so, should we allow the doctors to give medications that might facilitate a quicker, less painful birth? Then again, such drugs might lengthen labor and be dangerous for the baby. How would we know? The uncertainty quickly turned to fear that we might make the wrong decision.

Where once it was enough to listen to the wisdom handed down from one mother to the next, it had become important to consult an array of experts. The modern world had taught us to trust the professionals and to distrust hand-me-down advice, yet our postmodern ethos had taught us that even the expert opinion is not immune to overstatement, blind spots, and self-interest. So where did that leave us? We were too savvy to go back to Mom and Grandma and ask them how to raise our children. Yet neither could we pull a copy of Dr. Spock or Dr. Sears off the shelf and trust that this expert had properly and sufficiently mapped the terrain of childbirth and parenting.

Parenting is an arena of fear and anxiety in part because family life in general lacks cultural consensus about norms and standards. It's not just that we don't know if we're "getting it right," but that we don't even know what "right" would look like. And while experts can be very helpful in certain cases (I'm happy to go to a medical expert when my child is sick), when the experts disagree we are left with an uncertainty that magnifies fear.

In the absence of agreement about "good parenting," we find solace in "safe parenting." We don't let the nurses take our baby to the hospital nursery, because we've heard stories of babies getting mixed up or even stolen. Sure, it's unlikely, but it happens—we saw it on the news. And what about vaccinations? Can they cause autism? Wasn't there a Miss America candidate who became deaf because of a vaccination? (The answers to the last two questions are No and No.) We baby-proof the house with the latest safety products. We worry about toxins in our foods and plastic bottles. Ordinary living becomes fraught with reminders of extraordinary dangers.

Even sleeping poses a threat. The SIDS (Sudden Infant Death Syndrome) awareness campaign has undoubtedly done good things, but it has also extended our fearfulness into a time when we should find rest. As Frank Furedi, a sociologist at the University of Kent, notes, "The relentless publicity that surrounds crib death produces anxieties that are completely disproportionate to the scale of the problem."[1] When my wife and I became parents in 1999, the SIDS rate had fallen by over 50 percent since 1983. And from 1990 to 2017, the rate in the United States dropped further from 130 deaths to 35 deaths per 100,000 live births.[2] The SIDS Institute describes the syndrome as "very rare," yet for many parents the anxiety about SIDS far exceeds its likelihood.

In the midst of these fears, the marketplace steps forward to offer solutions—for a price. Child safety has become a lucrative industry in part because legitimate fears are heightened and manipulated. When good parenting is replaced by safe parenting, child rearing is easily captured by consumption—we may not be able to buy goodness, but we can buy safety. And if a given product claims to make your child safer, how do you refrain from buying it without seeming to say, "I'm not interested in my child's safety"? Yet where does it end? Being locked in a padded room is very safe, but it's hardly a life.

The themes of risk, safety, and the limits of parental control show up in the Pixar film *Finding Nemo*. Having lost his wife and a nestful of eggs to a shark attack, the clownfish Marlin makes it his mission to preserve his only remaining child, Nemo, from all danger. At one point he says to his friend Dory: "I promised him I'd never let anything happen to him." To which Dory replies, "Huh. That's a funny thing to promise." "What?" "Well, you can't '*never* let anything happen to him.' Then nothing would ever happen to him. Not much fun for little [Nemo]."[3] At some point our preoccupation with safety can get in the way of living full lives. Fear can poison a host of good and life-giving activities that we once took for granted, like taking a walk in the woods, playing in the sun, or swimming in the ocean.

The problem with these fears is not that they lack any basis in reality, but that we can become so overwhelmed by unlikely dangers that our parenting energy goes into avoiding threats rather than seeking healthy growth. We direct our energy toward a minimalist credo: "Allow no harm." But it is not enough just to keep our children safe. Their physical safety is a backdrop against which we as parents need to help them discover the joy of living, the thrill of new experiences, a robust engagement with the world around them, a dynamic relationship with the God who made them. All of this can easily be squelched when we parent out of fear. Parents need to create space for our children to explore and take risks in the process of growing, learning, and developing. We want our children to grow into adults who are expansive and generous rather than fearful and constricted, yet the culture of fear routinely squelches such an extravagant embrace of life.

As an antidote to fearful parenting, a "free-range kids" movement has emerged. In contrast to the helicopter parents who hover to keep all harm at bay, these parents are trying to give kids space to explore, make mistakes, and discover their freedom. Lenore Skenazy ignited the conversation by writing about her decision to let her nine-year-old ride the subway alone in New York City.[4] To fearful parents, such behavior seemed reckless, and she heard all about why she was a bad parent. But her message has resonated with many and created a healthy conversation about the right balance of risk and safety in good parenting.[5]

## Marketing, Media, and Fear

The fears associated with childhood and parenting are only one subset of the broader anxiety that assails us. Fear has long been a profitable sidekick for marketers and news agencies. When *Newsweek* publishes an article titled "That Little Freckle Could

Be a Time Bomb,"[6] and when local news anchors lead into stories with the words, "Why drinking too much water could send you to the emergency room,"[7] we can be sure that fear has become a bottom-line issue. We are surrounded by fear to the extent that we are surrounded by people who profit from fear.

This may help explain why our fears do not often correspond to the actual level of risk. For instance, Furedi observes, "Far more people die from an inadequate diet than from the widely publicized presence of toxic residues in food. . . . Clearly, the risks that kill you are not necessarily the ones that provoke and frighten you."[8] According to the Centers for Disease Control and Prevention, the top two causes of death in the United States by far are heart disease and cancer.[9] Yet these are not what we are most afraid of, or at least not in the same way we are afraid of immigrants, terrorists, pedophiles, road rage, school shootings, plane wrecks, risky strangers, and killer bees.[10]

Although we are in a time of heightened fear, our world is no more dangerous now than fifty, a hundred, or a thousand years ago. The dangers have changed—no one had to worry about plane crashes a hundred and fifty years ago—but in general we (at least "we" in the developed world) are living longer, healthier lives than ever before.[11] Consider how many serious illnesses, such as polio and smallpox, have been eradicated or significantly diminished in the last century. Those who think air travel has increased our risk should consider the dangers associated with traveling long distances by horse and buggy. Those who think youth are more violent today than ever should know that in 1850 New York City recorded over two hundred gang wars, most fought by adolescent boys.[12] Our present dangers are for the most part perennial dangers. Yet we imagine ourselves to be more threatened than ever.

Over the last quarter century, the rates of violent and property crime in the US have fallen over 50 percent. Yet surveys show that public perceptions of crime do not track with the data. Year after year, more than half of Americans believe that crime rates are rising even as they decline.[13] What accounts for this perception? One possible answer is what communications scholar George Gerbner called the "mean world syndrome." In his years of research on television violence, he found not so much a direct link between TV violence and real-world violence as a link between TV violence and exaggerated fear. Because we witness so much brutality, both on TV dramas and on news programs, we come to believe that the world is a scary and ominous place filled with violent predators. "Our surveys tell us," Gerbner writes, "that the more television people watch, the more they are likely to be afraid to go out on the street in their own community, especially at night. They are afraid of strangers and meeting other people. A hallmark of civilization, which is kindness to strangers, has been lost."[14] Indeed, it seems that the real effect of viewing violence is not a direct tendency to become violent (though that may be the indirect result) as much as a propensity to become fearful.

Another reason we are a more fearful culture today is that some people have incentives and means to heighten, manipulate, and exploit our fears. Fear is a strong motivator, and so those who want and need to motivate others—politicians, advertisers, media executives, advocacy groups, even the church—turn to fear to bolster their message. I call this the "fear for profit" tactic, and it is rampant. We have become preoccupied with unlikely dangers that take on the status of imminent threats, producing a culture where fear determines a disproportionate number of our personal and communal decisions. The sense of ever-increasing threats can overwhelm our ability to evaluate and respond proportionately to each new risk; thus, we allow fear to overdetermine our actions.

TV news, talk radio, and news websites bombard us with a kind of fearmongering that follows a distinct pattern. First, they present a hyped-up teaser, usually a variation on the "what you don't know might kill you" theme. "Coming up next, the story of a person who [fill in sensational catastrophe]. Find out how you can avoid becoming the next victim." Beginning with the story of a shocking "real-life" catastrophe, these stories continue by discussing this danger with a few "specialists" and end with helpful tips about how the rest of us can avoid this horrible fate. One such episode examined the problem of patients catching fire on the operating table when a surgical instrument ignites oxygen from a face mask.[15] The story gives the impression that this is a danger that could happen to any of us, yet this tragedy happens only once out of every 270,000 surgeries (about 0.0004 percent of the time). Still, we are told that this happens "more often than you might think"—a claim that is probably true but only because most of us were unaware that it happened at all.[16] The story creates a false sense of danger as a way of promoting the program.

Why do marketers and the media like to stir up fear? Fear, like sex, is one of our basic instincts. Both fear and sex move us to act; just as sex sells, so does fear. If marketers can tap into our fear, they can sell us a product to calm it, whether the product is a news story or an alarm system. While many have argued that the news media has either a liberal or a conservative bias, it may be that the bigger problem is the profit-making bias.[17] A drive for profit affects both the selection of news stories and the angle of coverage.

But news programming hasn't always been driven by profit. When broadcasting began in the 1930s, the US government allowed for-profit companies to control the public airwaves.[18] There was no US equivalent to Britain's nonprofit BBC (British Broadcasting Corporation). In return for using a public resource (the airwaves) for making a private profit, these companies had to show that they were providing a public service. The FCC could challenge the license of any broadcaster on the basis of its public service record. Broadcasters were happy to show that they were losing money on news as a form of public service (while making loads of money through their other divisions), thus defending against any FCC challenge. But with the deregulation of broadcasting that began in the 1980s, "the FCC largely abandoned the practice of challenging licenses on public service grounds."[19] The rise of competition from cable companies further contributed to the demand that network news shows not lose money. Thus, news-for-profit has rapidly expanded in the last several decades. Corporate owners of news companies hire consulting firms to conduct surveys and do market research to determine what stories will boost ratings. The results are passed along to the news divisions, who are told, as one executive put it, "what they ought to be covering and how they ought to be covering it."[20] News that is driven by a profit motive has to have ratings that can create advertising revenue. This is achieved through disproportionate coverage of the sensational and the shocking, which only intensifies our sense of fear.

Of course, not all of our fears have to do with death and loss. We also fear failure and rejection. These fears haunt our relationships and our work lives. We are targeted by advertising that depicts unrealistic body images and then offers to sell a product that will relieve our fear of inadequacy: buy this magazine with ten tips for greater beauty, better sex, happier relationships; buy this diet drink or protein supplement to get the body you want. In addition, we are sold items that promise to increase our sense of social worth: buy this car to appear successful; buy this craft beer to prove you have good taste; buy this phone to impress your friends. The social-media-driven fear of missing out (FOMO) leads us to compare our experiences with the carefully curated presentations of our friends and family. And the more time we spend on social media comparing our lives to others, the more money those sites make. Marketers excel at the creation and manipulation of what is "cool," "hip," "sexy," and "successful," and in so doing they tap into our fears of rejection and failure.

## Politics and Fear

Perhaps the most pervasive fear-for-profit enterprise is modern politics. With the first televised debate between Kennedy and Nixon in 1960, politics in the US changed forever. Campaigns came to look more and more like advertising, and the same fear-based strategies were employed by both. Over time the game plan of many campaigns came to be: if you can't woo voters, scare them. A few examples will suffice.

The notorious elect-Dukakis-and-murderers-like-Willie-Horton-will-roam-the-streets ads during the 1988 presidential campaign exploited fear to bolster George H. W. Bush's run. Horton, an African American man, had raped and murdered a White woman while on furlough from prison through a program put in place while Michael Dukakis was governor of Massachusetts. The ad painted Dukakis, the Democratic candidate, as "soft on crime" while exploiting racist stereotypes of the dangerous Black man and the vulnerable White woman. Lee Atwater, Bush's campaign manager, said the goal of the ad was to "make Willie Horton [Dukakis'] running mate." He later apologized, saying that the statement "makes me sound racist."[21]

The fear of crime has long been a mainstay of political campaigning, even when crime rates were dropping and other issues were far more pressing. In the quiet, relatively crime-free town where I used to live in northeastern Pennsylvania, election time brought a fear-driven media blitz. As the first Tuesday of November approached, a spate of television commercials warned senior citizens about the dangers of crime. The candidates promised to protect seniors through "harsh sentencing" of offenders. The fact that *seniors* were being targeted by the ads was a bit odd, since Justice Department reports showed that "people over 65 are less likely than any other age group to become victims of violent crime."[22] The actual threat did not correspond to the advertising hype, yet the real point was clear: seniors vote, and this kind of political advertising sought to mobilize seniors based on misrepresentations of their peril.

The terrorist attacks of September 11, 2001, planted fear at the heart of American politics for the rest of the decade. They shocked Americans out of the belief that "it could never happen here." After the initial astonishment and grief, fear morphed into anger, and the nation latched onto the rhetoric of revenge. Though the probability of dying in a terrorist attack on American soil was still incredibly low, the magnitude of these acts produced a pervasive anxiety that extended far beyond the actual threat.

Many have suggested that the Bush administration used the 9/11 strikes as an excuse to pursue initiatives, both foreign and domestic, that were already on the agenda but would have lacked public support apart from such a crisis. For instance, ousting Saddam Hussein had been a goal for some in the Bush administration prior to 9/11.[23] After the attacks, the administration invaded Iraq, despite the fact that Iraq was never directly linked to the hijackings. In his 2003 State of the Union address, Bush made the case for war: "Imagine those 19 hijackers with other weapons and other plans—this time armed by Saddam Hussein. It would take one vial, one canister, one crate slipped into this country to bring a day of horror like none we have ever known. We will do everything in our power to make sure that that day never comes."[24] Bush implied that Hussein was behind the September 11 attacks, but by all accounts this was not true.[25] Still, by linking the fear surrounding 9/11 to Hussein, Bush garnered public support for war by transferring our generalized fear of terror to a specific enemy who, as it turned out, had no real capacity to threaten the United States.

Of course, both major parties in US politics have used such tactics. During the 2004 presidential campaign, each party dressed itself in flag and uniform and portrayed the other party as dangerous. The Democrats were painted with the "soft-on-terror" brush, while the Republicans were decried as "reckless unilateralists." For a time after 9/11, it seemed that the entire arena of political conversation was reduced to the topic of security, the new alpha issue of single-issue politics. In 2004, Bill Clinton proclaimed, "Now, their opponents will tell you we should be afraid of John Kerry and John Edwards because they won't stand up to the terror. Don't you believe it. Strength and wisdom are not opposing values. They go hand in hand. They go hand in hand, and John Kerry has both. His first priority will be to keep America safe. Remember the scripture, 'Be not afraid.'"[26] Clinton drew upon the Bible to make his political claim, but in so doing he implied that overcoming fear had more to do with electing Kerry than with, say, trusting in God. Apparently, most Americans didn't believe him.

During Barack Obama's 2008 presidential campaign, conspiracy theories emerged that he was a Kenyan-born Muslim. These charges linked him to a trifecta of cultural fears: Black men, immigrants, and Islam. One of the most prominent voices in perpetrating these falsehoods was Donald Trump, whose capacity to spread lies and fear only increased once he took the White House in 2016. He became the fearmonger in chief. His go-to strategy has been to stoke fear of immigrants. In one of his oft-quoted rants, Trump declared, "When Mexico sends its people, they're not sending their best. . . . They're sending people that have lots of problems, and they're bringing those problems with us. They're bringing drugs. They're bringing crime. They're rapists. And some, I assume, are good people."[27] He has, at various times, described immigrants as criminals, rapists, invaders, and animals, creating the false impression that immigrants increase the crime rate—which is statistically untrue—and seeking to unite supporters against a common (false) enemy.[28] The border wall that he proposed during his campaign remains an icon of his fear-based presidency. And, to move from the malevolent to the ridiculous, Trump has argued that reliance on wind power is dangerous and naïve because one day the wind is going to stop blowing.[29] Trump is very good at making his supporters afraid of whatever issue or person he currently opposes—sometimes through lies, sometimes through ignorance, sometimes through exaggeration. But in each case, he puts on display the power of fear to produce political capital.

## Fear in Church

We have to add one more group to the list of those who use fear to consolidate power and influence opinion. As Episcopal bishop Paul Marshall observes, "Religious groups are particularly vulnerable to the kind of demagoguery that creates and capitalizes on fear. Many private religious empires in America have been built by religious entrepreneurs who play to people's fears. The airwaves are full of them."[30] Indeed, two favorite tools of evangelism have been the fear of hell and fear of the sword. The *conquistadores* notoriously converted indigenous peoples in Central and South America at sword point, and evangelists in the revivalist tradition have made ample use of hell to scare people into heaven.

Case in point, the website FearGod.com sells "Fear God" T-shirts promoting "shirt evangelism."[31] The site boasts: "The Fear God line of shirts contains bold scriptural truths. You won't be able to wear one of these shirts without telling someone about Jesus!" One shirt, sporting a skull with "666" imprinted on the forehead, warns, "It Is a Dreadful Thing to Fall into the Hands of the Living God: Repent or Perish." Ironically, the website suggests that wearing these shirts will draw "the lost" into conversations about God, because "people are more willing to listen when they are not threatened"! Such evangelistic products reflect the worst melding of Christianity and the market—using fear to gain religious and financial profit at the same time.

In many ways, the Christian subculture of books, music, concerts, festivals, schools, kitsch, and clothing relies on fear. Christian author and church planter Spencer Burke explains: "Believing that the world is an evil place to raise our children, we take a variety of steps to insulate ourselves from that reality. We watch Christian videos, read Christian books, and listen to Christian music. Why? Because we deem these items to be 'safe.'"[32] Some Christians would rather retreat to a Christ-saturated subculture than live in a complex, gray-shaded world.[33] A favorite slogan for Christian radio stations is "safe for the whole family." Such a tagline may calm fearful listeners, but it hardly reflects the Jesus who says dangerous things like "take up your cross and follow me."

The irony is that Christian subculture reproduces secular culture at its most problematic: its commitment to defining all life choices as consumer choices. As we have seen, fear often drives consumption in the hope that some new product will make us safer. Christian marketing exploits the same manipulative practices, suggesting that a particular product or a style of consuming will make us safer. We pretend to risk engagement with the world by mimicking the culture's trends in music, fashion, and technology, when all we are doing is covering the rough edges of real life with a smooth coat of Jesus.

And the problem is not relegated to conservative Christian subculture. Barbara Brown Taylor has observed that the church in all its forms "is a major player in the North American culture of fear. . . . Given the historical dominance of Protestant Christianity in this country, the popularity of civil religion, and the wedding of apocalyptic vision with national goals, . . .

it seems to me that 'a counter-cultural people of hope' may find themselves in the peculiar position of countering their own local church cultures."[34] This is just as likely to be true of a mainline congregation as it is of a fundamentalist T-shirt-selling business.

Christians tempted to give in to fear will find good guidance in the words of Swiss theologian Hans Urs von Balthasar. "The Word of God guarantees an objective distance from those Christian prophets of doom, who apply their misplaced melancholy and radicalism to the task of announcing the immediate and total demise of everything that is of lasting importance in the Church today."[35] We need a similar kind of "objective distance" from those in the church who would use fear to shore up either civil religion or a triumphalist Christian subculture.

## Following Jesus

In sum, politicians, media outlets, advertisers, and even religious leaders have a profit motive for exacerbating and sustaining our fears. This profit may come in the form of money, viewership, filled pews, influence, or power, but in each case we are encouraged to fear the wrong things or to fear the right things in the wrong way. Our anxiety drives us to act in ways that override other moral concerns. We spend our money based on fear rather than stewardship. We make political decisions based on fear rather than the common good. We participate in religious life based on fear rather than love.

We need some clear, sensible reflection on fear—how to acknowledge it without being manipulated by it, how to resist it without assuming we should (or could) be fearless, how to receive it as a gift without letting it dominate our lives. This is especially important among Christians who seek to follow Jesus, for Jesus does not promise safety. Following the teachings of Jesus will involve risky practices like clothing the naked, visiting the prisoner, caring for the sick, welcoming the stranger, and feeding the hungry (Matt. 25:31–46). Following Jesus will mean walking in the way of the cross, the way of self-giving love. The apostle Paul describes this vocation in his second letter to the Corinthians: "For while we live, we are always being given up to death for Jesus' sake, so that the life of Jesus may be made visible in our mortal flesh" (2 Cor. 4:11). Such risky discipleship is hardly "safe."

Of course, we have to be careful not to glorify risk, suffering, or powerlessness in a way that simply reinforces oppression. As Richard Hays cautions, "The image of the cross should not be used by those who hold power in order to ensure the acquiescent suffering of the powerless. Instead, the New Testament insists that *the community as a whole* is called to follow in the way of Jesus' suffering."[36] Christian discipleship will mean surrendering the power that masquerades as security in order to love the neighbor and welcome the stranger. It will mean avoiding the safe path in order to pursue the good. But in a culture of fear, we find such risks all the more difficult, since we naturally close in on ourselves when we face danger. How can we maintain the posture of the open hand toward a world that scares us? The following chapters will provide resources for living into the joyful freedom of those children of God who have put fear in its place.

## QUESTIONS FOR DISCUSSION

1. Can you think of ads, political commercials, social media campaigns, or news stories that create and manipulate fear? Do you think they work? If so, why do they work?

2. How has fear shaped your life? Do you have memories of being taught to fear as a child? If so, do you think

these fears taught you to live with proper care, or did they distort your view of the world?

3. George Gerbner claims that too much TV and news media creates a "mean world syndrome." Does this seem true of your experience or that of people you know?

4. Make a list of things you fear. Which ones would you describe as legitimate fears—those that help you avoid actual, present dangers? Which fears would you describe as constructed or manipulated fears—those that arise from some outside source (media, religion, politics) that wants to profit from your fear?

5. How can we avoid being manipulated by fearmongering? What tactics of resistance might we employ to ward off the fearful messages we receive every day?

6. The church has at times used fear of hell as a means of evangelism ("believe in Jesus, or go to hell") and as a way of keeping its members morally upright ("avoid sin, or you will go to hell"). How might we address the temptation of the church to use fear to control or manipulate?

## 2

# Fear and the Moral Life

If fear is, in fact, culturally pervasive and politically inescapable, the question arises: What does all of this fear do to us? What kind of people do we become if we are fed a steady diet of dread? How does fear affect our moral lives?

Perhaps we may begin answering these questions with another question: Why speak of fear as a *moral* issue? If fear is an emotion, how can we say that an emotion is good or bad? We don't experience emotions as chosen but as simply arising from within or washing over us. Popular wisdom tells us, "Your feelings are not good or bad, they're just feelings." How, then, can we speak of them as being appropriate or inappropriate, moral or immoral?

Theologian Simon Harak gives examples that show that emotions are not always neutral. "It is somehow wrong," he observes, "not to feel revulsion at rape, or to stay forever angry with imperfect parents. It is somehow right to rejoice at a friend's success, or to be moved by the plight of an abused child. So it seems upon reflection that our passions can be morally praise- or blameworthy."[1] The Christian tradition tells us that the proper ordering of our passions (including fear) helps shape character. If we wish to develop the virtues of courage and hope, we need to learn what to fear and how much to fear it. But we can do this only when we recognize that our emotional responses are largely socially conditioned.

Though the capacity to fear may be innate or prewired, the specifics of what we fear, when we fear, and how much we fear are largely learned. Scientific studies have shown this to be true in other animals; for instance, if a mother rat is made to be fearful and anxious during pregnancy, the baby rats will exhibit fearful and anxious behavior as well. And if new baby rats are introduced to this fearful mother, they too will begin to exhibit fearful behavior.[2]

Researchers Andreas Olsson and Elizabeth Phelps describe how humans socially learn fear. "You might fear a particular neighborhood because you were assaulted there, because you saw someone being assaulted there, or because someone told you an intimidating anecdote about a similar crime there." Thus, "fears can be acquired through direct experiences or indirectly through social transmission. In all cases, your fear of the locality might express itself similarly, such as by avoidance of the locality and increased autonomic arousal when approaching it. These responses might serve you well. However, if the experienced assault was a one-time event, the observed event a scene in a movie, or the anecdote a distortion of reality, your responses might disrupt normal functioning, especially if the neighborhood was your home."[3] Our passions are not simply given but also formed. Thus, we can learn to feel the passions in the right way, at the right time, and to the right extent—to rejoice rightly at the triumph of the good, to lament rightly in the face of suffering, and to feel anger rightly in the presence of cruelty.

Fear is not evil. It is not a vice (more on this in the next chapter). But excessive or disordered fear can tempt us to cowardice, recklessness, and rage. It can also inhibit other virtues such as hospitality, peacemaking, and generosity. Martin Niemöller was a German Lutheran pastor who opposed Hitler at a time when many Christians supported him. As a young man in 1933, Niemöller met with Hitler "as part of a delegation of leaders of the Evangelical Lutheran Church. . . . Niemöller stood at the back of the room and looked and listened. He didn't say anything. When he went home, his wife asked him what he had learned that day. Niemöller replied, 'I discovered that Herr Hitler is a terribly frightened man.'"[4] While fear itself is not evil, disordered fear can certainly breed and justify great evil.

## Attack or Contract

Fear is a moral issue insofar as it shapes the kind of people we become. And the kind of people we become has a lot to do with how we see the world around us. Our judgments about what is going on in the world and how to interpret events help us define proper actions. H. Richard Niebuhr went so far as to say that the first question of ethics is not "What is right?" or even "What is good?" but rather "What is going on?"[5] Before we can apply a rule, embody a virtue, or seek an outcome, we must interpret what is happening around us. Thus, in order to live well, we need to know how God is involved in history. To use Niebuhr's terms, the moral life is centered on the "fitting" response to the pattern of God's activity in the world.

But what if we are unable to see God's hand in our lives or the world around us? What if, in a postmodern world, we are less likely to see a story in history and more likely to see randomness, chaos, and threat? Niebuhr seemed to recognize that for many it was becoming harder to see God at work in the world. "We see ourselves surrounded by animosity," he writes. "Hence the color of our lives is anxiety, and self-preservation is our first law."[6]

In a culture of fear, the short answer to "What is going on?" is "We are at risk" or "We are in danger." Insofar as we accept that answer as our dominant description of the world, our lives will be shaped by self-preservation. Our moral vision becomes tunnel vision. Fear becomes the ambient background to our lives rather than a proper response to a discrete threat.

Psychologists have long taught us that fear in humans and animals provokes a "fight or flight" response. We either attack that which threatens us, hoping to overcome it, or we contract, hoping to avoid it. More recently, scientists have expanded the response palate to include "freeze." "Why do we freeze?" asks neuroscientist Joseph LeDoux. "It's part of a predatory defense system that is wired to keep the organism alive. . . . If you are freezing, you are less likely to be detected if the predator is far away, and if the predator is close by, you can postpone the attack (movement by the prey is a trigger for attack)."[7] Freezing is a form of contracting, a mode of avoidance that can be, at times, a very rational response to danger. But at other times, it's exactly the opposite of what is needed.

Thirteenth-century theologian Thomas Aquinas gives an illuminating explanation of the "contraction" that comes with fear. He writes, "Fear arises from the imagination of some threatening evil which is difficult to repel. . . . But that a thing be difficult to repel is due to lack of power . . . and the weaker a power is, the fewer the things to which it extends. Wherefore from the very imagination that causes fear there ensues a certain contraction in the appetite."[8] That is to say, fear is produced, in part, by our judgment that we are not strong enough to fight off a threat. Lacking power, we withdraw to conserve what strength and energy we have in order to fend off the danger. In this context, Aquinas uses the Greek term *systolē*, from which we get our English term *systolic*, referring to the contracting of the heart muscle as it pumps blood into the arteries. Fear, for Aquinas, can cause a contraction of the heart. By imagining some future evil, fear draws us in on ourselves so that we extend ourselves to fewer things. This, in turn, can hinder Christian discipleship, which calls us not to contract but to expand.

## The Ethic of Safety

When we make safety and self-preservation our highest goals, our moral focus becomes the protection of our lives and health. Security becomes the idol before whom all other gods must bow. In the past, when asked, "What is your chief goal?" Christians have answered, "Friendship with God" (Aquinas) or "To glorify God and enjoy him forever" (Westminster Catechism).[9] Today, I suspect many Christians—when being honest with themselves—would name "safety" or "security" as the primary good they seek.

Primary or highest goods serve the function of organizing our moral lives around the thing that is most important to us. The nature of a highest good is that we are willing to sacrifice other, lesser goods for the sake of that which is most valued. If we seek to love God and neighbor above all things (highest good), we might be willing to sacrifice certain creature comforts (lesser goods) in order to serve others in difficult circumstances. But if we seek safety above all things, we might be willing to sacrifice costly service to others in order to maintain the security we so deeply desire. And if safety is our highest good, then God cannot be.

Frank Furedi contends that fear has, in fact, "transform[ed] safety into one of the main virtues of society," making it an object of "worship." He warns us, "The disposition to panic, the remarkable dread of strangers and the feebleness of relations of trust have all had important implications for everyday life. . . . The outcome of these developments is a world view which equates the good life with self-limitation and risk aversion."[10]

Disordered fear has moral consequences. It fosters a set of shadow virtues, including suspicion, preemption, and accumulation, which threaten traditional Christian virtues such as hospitality, peacemaking, and generosity. Thus, our preoccupation with safety provides a temporary, though artificial, solution to our moral fragmentation. We may not be able to reach much agreement on hard issues like racism, immigration, abortion, war, health care, sex, and poverty. We may not agree on what virtues are most desirable for a full human life. But we can all agree on safety. The new ethic of safety provides a least-common-denominator morality. Surely we can all agree that we don't want to die. Surely we can all agree that safety is of utmost importance, since without life and health we cannot pursue any other goods. Our common fearfulness, then, takes on the appearance of a gift in that it creates a safety-based unity among a populace otherwise fragmented by political polarization, information bubbles, and technological isolation.

Such unity, however, is deceptive. Whenever there is a mass shooting, a common fear emerges among us, even if we live hundreds or thousands of miles away from the site of the tragedy. We sense that this could have been us. In a strange way it makes us one. We are then tempted to prolong this community built on fear, because as a fragmented people we want to linger in moments when we share a corporate mind and heart. In the end, however, such a community cannot last. Living only to prevent destruction, we neglect the calling to construct—to build a common life and to seek common goods. We are tempted to settle for a minimalist and passive ethic that says simply "avoid pain," "stay safe," and "be careful."

In our new ethic of safety, our moral language has been medicalized. Lacking consensus about what is good or right, we justify our ethical claims by an appeal to safety. Sex is one area where this is especially true. It is easier to define safe sex than good sex. And while good sex includes concerns about safety, safe sex often defers questions about what is good. In addition, the emphasis on keeping sex safe can set up sex as a fear-filled experience that is intrinsically dangerous. This revised sexual ethic of safety comes at the cost of a proper understanding of sex as a good gift that need not be feared. So when some Christians teach youth that what matters most is being safe and that either abstinence or condoms is the only sure way to be safe, they may gain some ground in controlling sexual activity, but in so doing they replace the expansive question "How can sex be good?" with the restrictive question "How can sex be safe?"

Traditional Christian ethics links sex and marriage not because sex is an intrinsically unsafe act but because sex finds its fulfillment in a context of promises that assure us of faithfulness and time. Regulating sex through fear may produce the restraint that some moralists hope for but only at the cost of misunderstanding sex and reinforcing the idea that moral decisions have to do with safety rather than risky self-giving. Christians want to do more than teach young people to engage or not engage in certain behaviors. We want to teach them how to love God, love themselves, and love others. When we overemphasize sexual safety, we fail to help them see sex as part of the great adventure (and risk) of living in a covenant that mirrors to the world the beauty and thrill of divine love. Our youth need the ability to trust, risk, and sometimes defer certain joys because they have come to understand their sexual lives in terms of a bigger vision than personal pleasure or personal safety.

When safety is worshiped as the highest good, we are tempted to make health and security the primary justifications for right action. We thus lead timid lives, fearing the risks of bold gestures. Instead of being courageous, we are content to be safe. Instead of being hopeful, we make virtues of cynicism and irony, which keep us a safe distance from risky commitments.

We are more likely to tell our children to "be careful" than to "be good." The extravagant vision that would change the world gets traded for the passive axiom "Do no harm."

Many people do bad things not because they are evil but because they are fearful. The relentless pursuit of safety produces uncharitable hearts, for we fear letting go of the goods that might protect us against an uncertain future. In the name of security we refuse to love our enemies, because we assume that if we do not answer violence with violence we will be forever victimized. We do not open our lives to strangers, fearing they will take advantage of our hospitality. Fear makes Jesus's ethic of risky discipleship look crazy, unrealistic, and irresponsible. Yet the "virtues" of the ethic of safety—suspicion, preemption, and accumulation—turn out to be vices in disguise.

## Suspicion: "Don't Talk to Strangers"

When my wife and I began talking to our children about strangers, we checked some books out of the library that dealt with the topic in fairly balanced ways. But the central message was clear: "Don't talk to strangers." Of course we wanted to protect our children, but we did not want to teach them to identify the stranger with danger. We wanted them to be careful *and* to learn that hospitality is a virtue.

At the time, there was an anticrime billboard near our neighborhood featuring McGruff the crime dog. The message read, "When you know your neighbors, the bad guys stand out." My first thought upon reading this was that it was a great idea to get to know your neighbors. This is good hospitality and has the added bonus of making us safer. But as I thought more about the message, it began to concern me. For one thing, it is impossible to know *all* your neighbors, so all you can really know is what your neighbors predominantly look like—White, Black, Latinx, wealthy, poor, old, young, walkers, drivers, and so on. The billboard asked us to equate the stranger—whoever did not look like one of us—with "bad guys." To be different is to be dangerous.

Suspicion becomes a virtue in the culture of fear. If we assume we are always at risk, we will always treat others as potential threats. The deadly results of such calculations can be seen clearly in the killing of Trayvon Martin, a seventeen-year-old African American youth shot and killed by George Zimmerman, a neighborhood watch coordinator in the gated community where Martin's relatives lived. In the eyes of Zimmerman, Martin did not look like the neighbors; he did not look like he belonged. And by the logic of stranger danger, he was treated as a threat. The fact that Zimmerman was acquitted based on an argument of self-defense suggests that the jury, which included no African Americans, agreed.

Furedi tells of a "Stranger Danger" campaign in Leeds, England, in 1988. Among the many messages that saturated the community was "One false move and you're dead." Looking at the effects such campaigns had on children, one study concluded, "We have created a world for our children in which safety is promoted through fear. The message of campaigns such as 'One false move and you're dead' is one of deference to the source of the danger. That such a world can be advertised without apparent embarrassment by those responsible for the safety of children, and without provoking public outrage, is a measure of how far the unacceptable has become accepted."[11]

The mentality that turns suspicion into a virtue has become a commonly accepted part of the American political landscape. After 9/11, airports became symbolic sites of security, where the suspicious stranger was presumed to be dangerous until proven otherwise. Beginning in January 2004, customs officers began photographing and fingerprinting all foreign visitors who entered the United States on a visa. In 2016 President Trump signed a travel ban suspending entry into the US from seven

Muslim-majority countries. Citizens of those countries were considered suspicious based solely on their nationality and, presumably, the religious identity attached to their nation. Such actions heighten the perception that certain foreigners—those who are least like White, Christian Americans—should be treated the same way police suspects are treated.

The treatment of the alien is an important biblical theme that suggests a very different response to strangers. After the exodus from Egypt and their return to the promised land, the Israelites found themselves facing dangerous enemies. Yet God commanded them, "When an alien resides with you in your land, you shall not oppress the alien. The alien who resides with you shall be to you as the citizen among you; you shall love the alien as yourself, for you were aliens in the land of Egypt: I am the LORD your God" (Lev. 19:33–34). Today we are quick to quote "love your neighbor as yourself"; we are less likely to remember God saying, "love the alien as yourself." We see biblical Israel enacting this welcome in the story of Ruth, where a Moabite woman is received, cared for, and gathered into the people of Israel.

This pattern of hospitality plays an important role in the New Testament, where Jesus shares meals with the aliens of his day—foreigners and sinners, the sick and the outcast. Jesus's disciples did not learn the lesson quickly. One day, on their way to Jerusalem, Jesus and his disciples entered a Samaritan village where they were not well-received. James and John knew just what to do: "Lord, do you want us to command fire to come down from heaven and consume them?" (Luke 9:54). But Jesus rebuked them. There is a tension in the biblical story between God's calling to welcome the stranger, the outsider, even the enemy, and the countertendency to exclude and destroy those whose difference or diffidence is perceived as a threat. Suspicion can look very much like a virtue when people are afraid.

## Preemption: "Do unto Others before They Do unto You"

The second shadow virtue of the ethic of safety is preemption. Preemption can take the form of fight, flight, or freeze. As flight or freeze, preemption resembles Aquinas's notion of "contraction," retreating from that which might harm us.

Some years ago, my wife and I attended a renewal-of-vows ceremony for some friends of ours. As the husband introduced the service, he admitted to the ways in which his own life had been far too determined by worry. He described the renewal of vows as "striking a blow against the empire of fear"—which, when I thought about it, made perfect sense. Marriage is an act that challenges our fears of abandonment, rejection, and failure. To marry is to confront those fears and refuse to allow them to determine one's relationship. To renew vows in a culture of fear is to close the back door of preemptive flight and to throw oneself totally and precariously into the hands of another and, for Christians, to throw oneself and the other totally into the hands of God. Preemptive flight can prevent us from engaging life and love, from taking risks and accepting adventure. It is characterized by our own lost opportunities and possibilities.

One writer tells such a story. "For the past 13 years, a few days each week, I practiced social distancing by living 200 miles from my husband, Michael—not because I didn't love him, but because I loved him so much. My fear: If I were to leave my old life behind to be with Michael, losing him would mean losing everything. For our entire marriage, he and I have lived as if we each had one foot on home base, hesitant to run toward each other, scared to be tagged out."[12] For fear of losing each other, they could not draw near.

When preemption takes the form of "fight" rather than "flight or freeze," we get preemptive attack. This can be seen most clearly in politics. Whenever America has been driven more by fear than hope, preemptive violence has become ordinary. We comfortably justify violence not only in the face of an actual threat but in the face of potential threats. Examples abound. Though the "doctrine of preemption" was not created by George W. Bush, he was the first to name it in 2002 as a determining principle in US foreign policy.[13] This doctrine expanded the justified use of violence exponentially, since strong suspicion alone could warrant a preemptive attack. The practice of holding and torturing prisoners in Guantanamo Bay was justified as preemptively necessary. Torturing someone to get information—not as a punishment but as an interrogation technique—was said to help prevent future terrorist attacks. The reality that this almost never produced useful information was secondary to the spectacle that delivered two messages to the American people: we are keeping you safe and we will stop at nothing to do it.[14] These political messages continued to provide a reason to keep Guantanamo Bay open long after it ceased to have a purpose.

The preemptive logic that stops at nothing to make people safe (even if that, in turn, makes people less safe) was on display after the Paris terrorist strike in November 2015. Responding to the attacks, Donald Trump affirmed, "We're going to have to do things that we never did before. And some people are going to be upset about it, but I think that now everybody is feeling that security is going to rule."[15] He then suggested that if Paris had less restrictive gun laws "it would've been a much, much different situation."[16] Trump was echoing Vice President Dick Cheney's sentiments after the 9/11 attacks when Cheney said, "We also have to work sort of the dark side, if you will. We're going to spend time in the shadows in the intelligence world. . . . And so it's going to be vital for us to use any means at our disposal, basically, to achieve our objective. . . . It is a mean, nasty, dangerous, dirty business out there, and we have to operate in that arena."[17] In the face of fear, preemptive violence helps us feel safe that those who might be dangerous will be struck before they can strike us. The moral horror of this sometimes threatens to break through, but it is easily diverted by claims that there is no alternative.

In the song "Devils & Dust," Bruce Springsteen, one of our great cultural commentators, explores what fear does to those entrusted with the task of violently assuring our safety. He imagines the plight of an American soldier guarding a military checkpoint. The song does not aim to judge the soldier but to lament what constant fear will do to a person's soul. Springsteen sings:

> I got my finger on the trigger
> But I don't know who to trust
> When I look into your eyes
> There's just devils and dust
>
> I got God on my side
> I'm just trying to survive
> What if what you do to survive
> Kills the things you love
> Fear's a powerful thing
> It can turn your heart black you can trust
> It'll take your God filled soul
> And fill it with devils and dust[18]

By the end of the song Springsteen alters the refrain from "Fear's a powerful thing" to "Fear's a dangerous thing," reminding us that the fear inside of us may become more dangerous than the threats outside of us.

The possibility that violence meant to calm our fears may actually "kill the things we love" became a reality for one man on a London subway on July 22, 2005. The incident occurred during the tense weeks after terror attacks rocked London's transportation systems and just one day after a second set of bombs failed to detonate. Jean Charles de Menezes, a Brazilian electrician working in London, was being tailed by plainclothes police officers as he made his way to work. As he entered the

Stockwell station the officers chased him down, brought him to the ground, and shot him multiple times in the head. Fearing he was a terrorist, the police had engaged a "shoot-to-kill protocol." This protocol defined certain circumstances in which officers were directed to shoot a suspect without warning if they thought he might be ready to activate a bomb.[19] The man, as it turned out, was simply an electrician making his morning commute.

The London police and the British government referred to this incident as a tragic mistake, but this is precisely what we should expect from a strategy of preemption. It is the predictable "collateral damage" of a preemptive protocol. The very nature of preemption is to strike before the other person has struck. Only after the fact can one know whether the other person was planning to strike or not. In this case he was not. At de Menezes's funeral, Cardinal Cormac Murphy-O'Connor cut to the heart of the matter when he urged people not to "surrender to a logic of fear."[20] Such logic turns the killing of innocents into a "tragic necessity," lamentable but acceptable if it helps us feel safe.

## Accumulation: "Save for a Rainy Day"

Another way in which the ethic of safety distorts our perceptions is by tempting those with resources to accumulate wealth in order to stave off misfortune. Beneath this is a set of legitimate fears: fear of losing jobs, fear that Social Security will run out of money, fear that health insurance will not cover expensive treatments or long-term care. So people come to believe that the more they have, the less they need to fear. They accumulate to try to secure themselves against an uncertain future. This is far different from greed, they tell themselves. This accumulation of wealth is often called "wise financial planning."

A friend who is a financial planner once told me and my wife that we would need more than $1 million to retire "comfortably"

(I laughed). I don't know what exactly she meant by "comfortably," but the word suggests something far less than extravagance. Indeed, the very matter-of-factness of the statement carried a subtle warning that if we didn't have a grand sum tucked away, we would live *uncomfortably* in our older years. But what does all that pressure to hit the million-dollar mark do to our ability to be generous here and now?

In the Lord's Prayer, Jesus teaches his followers to pray, "Give us this day our daily bread" (Matt. 6:11). Jesus does not encourage us to pray for tomorrow or the next day or for enough money to secure a grand retirement. Rather, he calls us to be content with God's provision for the day. Just a few verses later Jesus tells his followers, "Do not store up for yourselves treasures on earth" (v. 19). These teachings indicate that following Jesus will involve releasing our "stored-up" goods to those who have needs now so that we might be the means by which God gives to them their daily bread. Excessive fear closes us off from such vulnerability and from welcoming the daily gift of God's provision.

With our moral lives so deformed by fear, how can we hope to live as nonanxious recipients of God's gifts? It might seem that the best response would be to rid ourselves of fear entirely, to live as fearless people. But fearlessness, as I will show in the next chapter, is a temptation we need to resist.

## QUESTIONS FOR DISCUSSION

1. If fears are largely learned, how are they taught? Do we teach them consciously or unconsciously? Does this teaching come through family, school, culture, or all of the above? Do you have any particularly strong fears or phobias? Can you remember how you learned them?

2. Would you say that "safety" is the most important thing in your life? If not, what is it that you seek more than that?

3. Do you find yourself suspicious of other people as you go about your daily activities? What makes them seem suspicious?

4. How is preemption at work in your life or in the lives of those around you? How can we avoid having a preemptive mindset individually and as a culture?

5. How do you make judgments about accumulation? Do you believe there is such a thing as accumulating too much? Does saving for the future make you less likely to share your wealth in the present?

# 3

# Why Fearlessness Is a Bad Idea

The Brothers Grimm tell a peculiar tale of a boy who goes into the world to learn how to fear. He has little knowledge or skill, but he does have the odd trait of being unafraid of anything. When his father suggests that he learn something useful, he replies that he wishes to learn "how to shudder." So begins his journey to learn fear. What is most interesting about the story is that the boy is not only without fear; he is also without love or compassion. He can't relate to others in any identifiably human way. He throws an innocent man down the stairs of a church tower, leaves him lying crumpled in a corner, and goes home to bed. He beats an old man with an iron bar and seems utterly unmoved. When he grows up, he finally learns to shudder when his wife throws a bucket of cold water on him while he sleeps. He wakes up shouting, "Oh, what is making me shudder? . . . Yes, now I know how to shudder."[1]

You can understand why this tale is not among the Grimms' greatest hits. The ending is anticlimactic if not a total non sequitur, and it is not clear that the boy has learned to fear so much as to be startled. But the story is illuminating in that it correlates lack of fear with lack of love. The boy lacks fear *because* he lacks love, since those who love nothing fear no loss.

While fearlessness might appear to be desirable, this folktale suggests it may be a vice. We fear evil because it threatens the things we love—family, friends, community, peace, and life itself. The only sure way to avoid fear, then, is to love less or not at all. If we loved nothing, we would have no fear, but this would hardly be considered a good thing.

Some say that fear and love are opposites, that we encounter the world fundamentally from within one frame or the other. While I am sympathetic with the goal of becoming more loving and less fearful, I think the relationship between the two is more complicated. In fact, fear is the shadow side of love. Our response to living in a dangerous world ought not to be to do away with fear but to feel fear in the right way, at the right time, and to the right extent. Again, we can learn from Aquinas, who observed that "fear is born of love."[2] Because fear and love walk hand in hand, there is no way to eradicate one without losing the other. We would need to be concerned if we had no fear, for it would be a sign that we had no love. This helps explain why Aquinas calls fear a gift and fearlessness a vice.[3]

## Fear and Love

Fear can serve to awaken us to loves that have been neglected. In this way fear can be a gift. Fear exists at the nexus of love and limitation. We love much about our world, yet our power to preserve what we love is limited. Indeed, we participate in a web of life that includes growth and decay, birth and death, victory and defeat. Limitation is part of what it means to live as mortals in a created world. Limitation and mortality are not evil but are part of what Karl Barth called the "shadow side" of creation.[4] They are the shadows cast when the light of God's goodness shines upon a fragile and finite world. Love in a changing world casts a shadow that hints at inevitable loss. The larger the love, the larger the shadow. The larger the shadow, the larger the fear. While some amount of fear is normal and natural, we must not allow the shadow of loss to diminish our ability to love and enjoy what is present.

Augustine of Hippo, in his *Confessions*, reflects on the pain of love and loss as he remembers the death of a dear friend. He gives voice to feelings that are familiar to any who have lost those they love. "Everything I had shared with my friend turned into hideous anguish without him. My eyes sought him everywhere, but he was missing; I hated all things because they held him not, and could no more say to me, 'Look here he comes!' as they had been wont to do in his lifetime when he had been away." Like many who have faced loss, Augustine is tempted to reject love altogether, for every new love contains "the seeds of fresh sorrows." Then Augustine prays, "Turn us toward yourself, O God . . . for wheresoever a human soul turns, it can but cling to what brings sorrow unless it turns to you. . . . Yet were these beautiful things not from you, none of them would be at all. They arise and sink; in their rising they begin to exist and grow toward their perfection, but once perfect they grow old and perish."[5] Augustine recognizes that transience is built into the nature of a created world. Loss is inevitable. Only God does not change; only God is eternal.

Because love and loss are natural, so is fear. Fear is born of love, but it is also born of the knowledge that all loves are subject to decay and death. To love is to plant seeds of sorrow. And yet, recognizing our limitation can produce gratitude.

Sometimes it is when our loves are most threatened that we see them most clearly. Those who face near-death experiences or terminal illnesses often report that they grow to love their family and friends and appreciate everyday life all the more.

One survivor of the 9/11 attacks remarked, "I like this state. I've never been more cognizant in my life."[6] Such a response may seem strange at first blush, but it should not surprise us. Fear alerts us to love in a powerful way. It can focus our actions and clarify our priorities. Aquinas observes that "if the fear be moderate, without much disturbance of the reason, it conduces to working well, in so far as it causes a certain solicitude, and makes a man take counsel and work with greater attention."[7] Moderate fear can imbue one's life and work with a sense of seriousness and import. Perhaps this is why Benedict, the sixth-century monk, lists among his "instruments of good works" the injunction to "keep death daily before one's eyes."[8]

After he was diagnosed with terminal cancer, Joseph Cardinal Bernardin, archbishop of Chicago, wrote powerfully about the transformation he underwent. Spending time among cancer patients and others with serious illnesses, he discovered that "those in this community see things differently. Life takes on new meaning, and suddenly it becomes easier to separate the essential from the peripheral."[9] In a pastoral letter he notes that through his struggle with cancer, he "came to realize how much of what consumes our daily life is trivial and insignificant."[10] This altered gaze, this truthful seeing, can be a gift that arises out of our limitation and is fed by moments when fear reminds us both of our loves and of our fragility. Apart from a sense of threat and fear, we are sometimes lulled into a false security that leads us to take our loves for granted and thus to cease to rejoice in them and protect them. Fear alerts us to our loves because in fear we imagine our loves lost.

## Waking Up to Fear

The positive function of fear as an early warning system can help us understand why some particular fears should be respected or even elevated. These are not necessarily the fears that are most dominant in media, politics, or religion. One of the significant problems with misplaced fear is that it turns our attention away from real threats. As evidenced by broad scientific consensus, climate change may be the most comprehensive threat to human well-being. But fear of climate change is hard to muster, since its slow development across many generations makes the threat seem less imminent. It may be that in this case it would be wise to elevate the public fear given the level of threat climate change poses to life and well-being.

It is also true that those who have become the *objects* of fear have good reason to become fearful themselves. Latinx immigrants, Muslims, African Americans, and LGBTQ+ persons have all been on the receiving end of fearmongering campaigns. These campaigns claim to be about keeping "us" safe (where the "us" is often White, straight Americans). But what they do, in fact, is make those with less power feel even less safe. Howard Thurman perceptively identifies and describes the fear of the oppressed:

> Fear is one of the persistent hounds of hell that dog the footsteps of the poor, the dispossessed, the disinherited. . . . It is nowhere in particular yet everywhere. It is a mood which one carries around with himself, distilled from the acrid conflict with which his days are surrounded. It has its deep roots in the heart of the relations between the weak and the strong, between the controllers of environment in those who are controlled by it.
>
> When the basis of such fear is analyzed, it is clear that it arises out of the sense of isolation and helplessness in the face of the varied dimensions of violence to which the underprivileged

are exposed. Violence, precipitate and stark, is the sire of the fear of such people.[11]

Thurman captures the way that fear falls upon those who lack social and political power and who despite this (or because of this) are targeted by campaigns that portray them as a threat to others. In this case, the faithful response is not to counsel less fear but to address the causes of fear.

An important part of waking up to the injustices perpetrated on "the poor, the dispossessed, the disinherited" is recognizing the way fearmongering can become a self-fulfilling prophecy. For instance, it should not be a surprise that anti-Muslim discrimination is linked to Muslim radicalization in parts of the US.[12] The findings of one study "suggest pro-ISIS sympathy is most prevalent in communities with high levels of anti-Muslim sentiment."[13] In short, the political manipulation of fear can end up producing the very threats it purports to be confronting.

## Fear of the Lord

The idea that fear can be a natural warning sign of a real threat and a positive indicator of the value of our loves finds a parallel in the biblical concept of "the fear of the Lord." It is "the beginning of wisdom," says Proverbs 9:10; Isaiah 11:2 lists "the fear of the Lord" as a gift of the Spirit. Nonetheless, this phrase is widely misunderstood and can be used in ways that sound like anything but a gift. Biblical scholar Ellen Davis notes that upholding fear "as a healthy and necessary disposition toward God" represents for many modern readers "one of the most offensive things in the Old Testament."[14] One can understand why some people would take offense, given how appeals to the "fear of God" can be used to coerce and threaten.

First, we have to reconcile "fear of the Lord" with the God of grace who calms our fears and delivers us from evil. We are often told in Scripture *not* to fear precisely because God is with us: "God is our refuge and strength, a very present help in trouble. Therefore we will not fear" (Ps. 46:1–2). "Do not fear" is the message of Moses to the people of Israel (Deut. 31:6), of Isaiah to a destroyed Jerusalem (Isa. 40:9), of the angel Gabriel to Mary (Luke 1:30), of Jesus to Paul (Acts 18:9), and of Jesus to John on the island of Patmos (Rev. 1:17). We are told that "There is no fear in love, but perfect love casts out fear" (1 John 4:18). Why would we fear God if God is love, the source of our comfort and deliverance?

Yet at other times, Scripture suggests that the God who is love is the very one we should fear. Abraham is thus praised by the angel: "Now I know that you fear God" (Gen. 22:12). The words of Moses to the Israelites illustrate the paradox of fear in the Bible, "Do not be afraid; for God has come only to test you and to put the fear of him upon you so that you do not sin" (Exod. 20:20). Do not be afraid, he seems to say, because God has come to make you afraid.

What is going on here? Does God calm our fears or make us fearful? Jesus echoes this tension when he tells his disciples, "Do not fear those who kill the body but cannot kill the soul; rather fear him who can destroy both soul and body in hell" (Matt. 10:28). One might mistakenly assume that Jesus is saying we should not fear lesser, earthly fears precisely because we have a much bigger threat to worry about—God. But does it make any sense to speak of God as someone who threatens the good things we love? Are we meant to "fear" God in that way?

Davis notes that some Bible translators today render the phrase "fear of the Lord" as "reverence for the Lord." She agrees that "reverence is part of what the sages mean to commend to us," but she argues that this translation leaves too much out. "The writers are speaking first of all of our proper gut response to God," she writes. "Fear is the unmistakable feeling in our bodies, in our stomachs and our scalp, when we run up hard against the power of God. From a biblical perspective, there is nothing neurotic about fearing God. The neurotic thing is *not* to be afraid, or to be afraid of the wrong thing. That is why God chooses to be known to us, so that we may stop being afraid of the wrong thing. When God is fully revealed to us and we 'get it,' then we experience the conversion of our fear."[15] God wants to turn our fear away from worldly objects that only manipulate, control, and coerce us and to redirect it to the God whose power does not threaten our true good but sustains it.

Describing our experience of God as "fear" makes sense, then, when understood rightly. To return to Davis, "The time comes in every life—and more than once—when we are personally confronted with the power that spread out the heavens like a sequined veil, that formed us out of dust and blew breath into our lungs, that led Israel through the Red Sea on dry land and left Pharaoh's whole army floating behind. . . . 'Fear of the Lord' is the deeply sane recognition that we are not God."[16] Fear of the Lord, understood in this way, shares more in common with our sense of awe at something wondrously bigger than ourselves than it does with our anxiety in the face of evil.

Aquinas helpfully draws a distinction between "servile fear" and "filial fear." He explains "servile fear" by drawing on the analogy of a servant who does right because he fears the punishment of the master. Though this kind of fear might encourage us to do good, it should not be considered a "gift" from God, since it is tied too closely to worldly power. Aquinas's description of "filial fear," on the other hand, draws on the analogy of a parent and a child, a relation that is much more like that between God and humankind. This fear is based in love and affection and presumes that we know God not as a threatening judge but as a loving parent. As when children fear harming their relationship with their parents more than they fear being punished for doing wrong, a healthy fear of God arises from a proper desire not to be separated from God. Because we love God, we fear anything that would harm our relationship with God. So, filial fear can turn us from bad choices, because we recognize that what could be lost is something we love greatly. Understood in this way, the "fear of God" is a gift of the Holy Spirit that can help us resist evil and pursue the good.

## The Vice of Fearlessness

This view of fear challenges a good deal of conventional wisdom and pop psychology. One self-help rabbi goes so far as to write that "you must first abandon all thoughts that fear serves a useful purpose in your life. . . . You must accept that fear is not only harmful but evil, not only unhelpful but deeply destructive. Fear has not a single healthy application in any area of life. Period."[17] On the surface this may sound wise. But in practice we need to ask, What is the price we would have to pay for fearlessness?

Aquinas argues that we can become fearless in three ways: through a "lack of love" (loving nothing enough to fear its loss), through "dullness of understanding" (not knowing or acknowledging the danger or threat), or through "pride of soul" (refusing to believe that one is susceptible to loss).[18] In contemporary terms, we might think of these as "the security of detachment," "the bliss of ignorance," and "the pursuit of invulnerability."

As with the boy in the Grimm fable, one way to be without fear is through "the security of detachment," loving nothing enough to care if it is lost. After the death of his friend, Augustine was tempted to avoid love. I would imagine that most of us who have experienced significant pain or loss have felt tempted to seek refuge in this kind of fearlessness. Rather than live with the fear that we will be hurt once more, we build walls, resolving never to sow the seeds of sorrow again. We try to protect our hearts from pain, but in the process we shield ourselves from love. Our hearts are contracted, our relationships diminished. This posture of detachment comes at too high a price.

Another way to become fearless is through the "the bliss of ignorance." This kind of fearlessness can arise through a passive denial of the real dangers that exist or through willful ignorance that amounts to recklessness. And recklessness often disguises itself as courage. The difference is that courage does not lack fear altogether; it feels fear appropriately but does not allow fear to control one's life, diminish one's loves, or divert one's pursuit of the good. Recklessness, on the other hand, seeks to be fearless, producing a desire to create dangerous situations in order to experience and then overcome fear. A reckless fearlessness, however, does not overcome fear so much as give in to an uncritical fascination with fear.

The final path of fearlessness is "the pursuit of invulnerability." In his 2005 State of the Union address, President Bush asserted that one of our responsibilities "to future generations is to leave them an America that is safe from danger, and protected by peace. We will pass along to our children all the freedoms we enjoy—and chief among them is freedom from fear."[19] The sentiment here cannot be disputed, for of course we wish for our children to be free from fear. And yet what does it take to have no fear? The only way for government to ensure a freedom from fear is to make its people invulnerable. Aside from whether or not that is possible, what price would be paid in its pursuit?

The pride of soul that Aquinas talks about includes not only the "it can't happen to us" mentality of the wealthy elite and the superpowers but also the "it won't happen to us" mentality that drives an individual, community, or nation to become so powerful that it cannot not be threatened. But how could we possibly ensure freedom from fear unless we were able to destroy all imminent *and* potential threats? The price we pay is an unending war on every conceivable threat—imprisoning suspicious individuals without charges, detaining asylum seekers indefinitely without hearings, and setting aside the human rights of some to ensure the security of others.

We seek invulnerability because we fear the loss of what we love, but could it be that our attempts at invulnerability, whether on a national or a personal level, only destroy the things we wish to save?

## Detachment and Invulnerability

Detachment and invulnerability are well-worn strategies to avoid hurt. Writing about love, C. S. Lewis confesses that he is a "safety-first creature." "Of all arguments against love none makes so strong an appeal to my nature as 'Careful! This might lead you to suffering.'" But he recognizes in the lure of safety something that does not sound like Jesus. "When I respond to that appeal I seem to myself to be a thousand miles away from Christ. If I am sure of anything I am sure that His teaching was never meant to confirm my congenital preference for safe investments and limited liabilities. I doubt whether there is anything in me that pleases Him less. And who could conceivably begin to love God on such a prudential ground—because the security (so to speak) is better?"[20] Love does not commend itself on the basis of such calculations.

The tendencies in Christian theology toward dispassionate disengagement owe more to Stoicism and Neo-Platonism than to the New Testament. Jesus loves vulnerably as he weeps over the death of his friend Lazarus (John 11:35), and Paul writes of the sorrow he would have had if his friend Epaphroditus had died (Phil. 2:27). The link between love and fear is plain. If one is to love as God commands, one cannot seek to avoid fear through invulnerability. Lewis writes,

> To love at all is to be vulnerable. Love anything, and your heart will certainly be wrung and possibly be broken. If you want to

make sure of keeping it intact, you must give your heart to no one, not even to an animal. Wrap it carefully round with hobbies and little luxuries; avoid all entanglements; lock it up safe in the casket or coffin of your selfishness. But in that casket—safe, dark, motionless, airless—it will change. It will not be broken; it will become unbreakable, impenetrable, irredeemable. The alternative to tragedy, or at least to the risk of tragedy, is damnation. The only place outside of heaven where you can be perfectly safe from all the dangers and perturbations of life is Hell.[21]

There is no path by which faithfulness avoids fear, since love cannot avoid risk. To attempt it is to lose the very capacity to love that constitutes our salvation. "What if what you do to survive kills the things you love?" asks Springsteen. And, perhaps worse, what if what you do to survive kills your ability to love them?

## QUESTIONS FOR DISCUSSION

1. Do you agree that fear can be a gift? Have you (or someone you know) ever had an experience of fear that awakened you to your loves?

2. If every new love contains the "seeds of fresh sorrows," then why do we love at all? Why not just avoid love, avoid loss, and avoid fear?

3. How have you traditionally understood the biblical phrase "fear of God"? Do you think fearing God can be a gift?

4. Fearlessness is a problem not just because it robs us of the gifts fear can bring but also because of the price we pay to be fearless. Do you find yourself more tempted to avoid fear through "the security of detachment," "the bliss of ignorance," or "the pursuit of invulnerability"?

# 4

# Putting Fear in Its Place

I have long been curious about this line in the well-loved hymn "Amazing Grace": "'Twas grace that taught my heart to fear / And grace my fears relieved." Well, I've thought, which is it? Are we taught to fear or are we relieved of fear? Perhaps both. The hymn rightly suggests we need to be *taught* to fear, or, better put, we need to be taught to fear well. But this teaching of fear, according to the hymn, must come by grace, for only grace can give us the courage to fear as we should. Grace puts fear in its place. But what does this look like in practice?

We might begin with some left-brain strategies—rationally examining the relation of fear and threat. We might complement these with some right-brain strategies—developing practices of reflection and contemplation that loosen fear's grip on our soul.[1] While there is much to be said for understanding when and where fear is actually warranted, the truth is, it's hard to reason your way out of fear. No matter your ability to say, "This fear is irrational," the fear doesn't always obey the cease-and-desist order. Fear is an emotion that is not simply amenable to being told what to do.

We need both to understand fear better and to loosen the control fear exerts on our emotional lives. We need to find tools that will help us determine when fear is a natural warning sign and when it is a toxic tyrant that threatens our character and communities. Fear itself is not evil, but it can become such. Excessive or disordered fear can drain the joy out of life, can constrict our vision and feed our hatreds. Fear can cause us to love less because we fear too much the seeds of sorrow that inhabit every love. Excessive fear can rob our lives of playfulness, exploration, and adventure. Fear can be a gift, but it can also be a poison. How do we know the difference? How do we put fear in its place?

## Fearing *What* We Should Not

Here again, Thomas Aquinas helps us map the terrain of fear. Aquinas observes that fear arises from the imagination of a future evil (something that threatens the loss of something we love) that is both imminent and hard to resist.[2] It follows, then, that fear can be disordered in two basic ways.[3] We can fear *what* we should not, either because the threat is not in fact great or because what we fear losing is not something we should have set our heart on in the first place (like riches or power). Or we can fear *as* we should not; that is, we may fear a real threat but fear it excessively. Using Aquinas's definition, we can come up with a way of testing fear, so that we might become more reflective and less captive.

We fear *what* we should not in many ways. If, as Aquinas tells us, the thing we fear is a future evil that is imminent, is of great magnitude, and threatens a loss of something we rightly love, then to fear what we should not would be to fear an object that does not in fact include all of these characteristics. We might

62

wrongly fear (a) an evil object that is imminent (present or fast approaching) but not of great magnitude—that is, not so very big after all and thus easily repelled; (b) an evil object that is of great magnitude but is not imminent and thus not a present threat; (c) something that is of great magnitude and imminent but is not really an evil object; or (d) an evil object that is imminent and of great magnitude but imperils only our love of an unhealthy attachment. When we use Aquinas's definition as a benchmark, then we are on our way to putting fear in its place.

Let's examine these criteria more closely. First, we might fear something that is imminent but not of great magnitude. This is the stuff of phobias: fear of spiders, heights, crowds, or small places. Phobias involve fearing excessively something that is part of everyday life that does not pose a significant threat. While phobias are powerful and can be destructive, they are not signs of real threats and so can be treated the way we would treat other unhealthy thoughts or beliefs.

Second, we might fear an evil object that is of great magnitude but is not in fact an imminent threat, such as shark attacks or lightning strikes. Aquinas writes, "Since fear arises 'from the imagination of future evil' [Aristotle, *Rhetoric* 2.5] . . . whatever removes the imagination of the future evil removes fear also. Now it may happen . . . that an evil may not appear as about to be [that is, may not appear imminent]. . . through being remote and far off: for, on account of the distance, such a thing is considered as though it were not to be. Hence we either do not fear it, or fear it but little."[4] So, one way to test our fear is to ask whether the evil we fear is far off or close at hand. For if an evil is "remote and far off," even if it is of great magnitude, we need fear it either not at all or very little.

This insight is important in our global village, where evils that are far off find their way into our homes and thoughts through news media, social media feeds, or NPR on the morning commute. Notifications that come 24/7 on our phones make sure that natural disasters, wars, and political unrest that once would have been known about only locally are now shared across the globe in seconds. In this way our imaginations bring everything close. They bring close evils that are in fact far away, thus making us fear when in fact we need not.

As noted in chapter 1, George Gerbner's "mean world syndrome" suggests that something similar happens with television. His findings show that "if you are growing up in a home where there is more than, say, three hours of television per day, for all practical purposes you live in a meaner world—and act accordingly—than your next-door neighbor who lives in the same world but watches less television."[5] How easy it is for us to misjudge the imminence of danger when the stories we are watching normalize violence and threat. This is not to say that every binge-worthy drama is a bad influence, only that we need to be attentive to the ways dramatic depictions of ruthless characters and menacing situations can lead us to misjudge the world around us.

The failure to discern the imminence of a threat also seems to be related to the magnitude of the threat. If the magnitude of an evil object is great, as is the case with weapons of mass destruction, we easily lose perspective as we attempt to judge its imminence. Because of the magnitude of the evil, we are tempted to fear it even if it is remote. Indeed, we are tempted to cease altogether making a distinction between evil that is close at hand and evil that is far away. US military engagement in the Middle East has long been predicated on building a sense of imminent threat even though the violence in that region has rarely reached US soil.

A third way in which we might fear what we should not is to fear an object that may be of magnitude and imminent but is not actually an evil object. For example, look at the ways fear operated in the long-standing debate over same-sex marriage before it was legalized in the US in 2013. This issue was certainly one of great magnitude—for the couples themselves, who waited decades to be recognized, for US politics and culture, and for churches that were enmeshed in controversies. And the issue was imminent, close at hand—both temporally pressing and relationally urgent. The question, however, is whether the legalization of same-sex marriage was a proper object of fear. That is, even for those who believed that the church could not support same-sex marriage, was fear the proper response?

Those who described their opposition to same-sex marriage as a "defense of marriage" seemed to imply a threat to something we properly love: marriage. But was there any evidence that legalizing same-sex marriage would harm heterosexual marriages? Indeed, such a claim seems counterintuitive, since it suggests that same-sex couples who wish to enter publicly into faithful lifelong covenants are in fact a threat to faithful lifelong covenants. Could it even happen that visible, faithful same-sex relationships lived with integrity and love would spur on heterosexual marriages to greater faithfulness? There is no logical reason to assume that allowing same-sex marriage would threaten traditional heterosexual marriage. Like the fear of interracial marriage, prohibited by law until 1967, the fear of same-sex marriage seems to have been driven largely by a desire to keep a particular set of people on the outside of social legitimacy. Thus, fear of same-sex marriage crosses over two types of misguided fear: (1) it fears a loss of something—marriage—that is not actually threatened, and (2) it fears losing heterosexual privilege, which is not a good worth loving.

This leads into the fourth way in which we might fear what we should not—to fear an evil object that does, in fact, threaten something we love, but something that we *should not* love. Aquinas calls this "worldly fear," since it is based on "worldly love"—that is, "the love whereby a man trusts in the world as his end."[6] This kind of fear turns us from God, since our fear of losing worldly loves makes us cling more tightly and attend more closely to them. When we love money, power, possessions, privilege, fame, leisure, or status, we fear their loss and focus more energy on their preservation. Though we often imagine that the accumulation of worldly goods makes us more secure, Aquinas points out that such accumulation tends to make us more afraid, since the more we have, the more we have to lose. He notes that "inordinate fear is included in every sin; thus the covetous man fears the loss of money, the intemperate man the loss of pleasure, and so on."[7] This insight is worth repeating: "inordinate fear is included in every sin." Thus, the wealthy, the powerful, and the privileged, who have the greatest capacity to fend off impending evils, are rarely less fearful and often more so than those who have less.

## Fearing *as* We Should Not

Fear can also become "disordered" when we fear *as* we should not—that is, when we fear *excessively*. In this case we may well fear things worth fearing, like divorce and heart disease, both of which are statistically common, or death itself, which is certain. But if we fear divorce, heart disease, or even death excessively, then we no longer fear well.

So how do we know when fear is excessive? According to Aquinas, "Reason dictates that certain goods are to be sought after more than certain evils are to be avoided. Accordingly when the appetite shuns what the reason dictates that we should endure rather than forfeit others that we should rather seek for, fear is inordinate and sinful."[8] Aquinas gets a bit complicated here, but he's simply saying that we fear excessively when we allow the avoidance of evil to eclipse the pursuit of good. When we fear excessively, we live in a mode of reacting to and plotting against evil rather than actively doing what is right. Excessive fear causes our scope of vision to narrow, when it needs to be enlarged.

Aquinas goes on to discuss the fear of losing material things. From what I have said so far, one might imagine that there is never a case in which such fear is justified. But Aquinas says otherwise. It is not always wrong to fear the loss of our possessions. This is true for two reasons.

First, says Aquinas, losing money or power makes us feel that we have fewer defenses against threats to our deeper loves. Aquinas asks "whether defect is the cause of fear." By "defect" he means a lack of something like money, strength, or friends. He answers that these defects *can* be a cause of fear, because what we fear ultimately are those evils that are not easily repelled, and "it is owing to some lack of power that one is unable easily to repulse a threatening evil."[9] In this sense, then, defect, or lack, is a kind of second-level fear, a fear that one will not have the resources to stave off the threat. So, according to Aquinas, we are not wrong to fear the level of "defect" that would make us vulnerable to future evil. For instance, we rightly fear an economic downturn if we lack the financial savings necessary to feed and care for ourselves or our children. We rightly fear old age if we lack family and friends who will support us and stay by our side.

Second, Aquinas turns to Augustine to remind us that although "temporal things are goods of the least account," they are nonetheless "goods." He continues, "Hence their contraries are indeed to be feared; but not so much that one ought for their sake to renounce that which is good according to virtue."[10] That is, we must not protect our possessions at the expense of more important goods. So it is not wrong to fear the loss of one's home, but it is wrong to fear the loss of one's home so much that one limits hospitality. Gated communities might, then, represent a kind of disordered love in which the desire to protect the lesser good of one's property leads a person to reject the greater good of hospitality.

As noted above, having excessive fear tends to make us attack or contract. Thus, one way of testing whether our fear is excessive is to ask to what extent we have begun to turn in on ourselves or lash out at others. Has our fearful aggression caused us to ignore or interpret away Jesus's call to love the enemy? Has our contraction begun to stifle our joy? Has our commitment to self-preservation caused us to turn our backs on those who need us?

Fear is related to love in that when we love, we fear the loss of that love. Joy is also related to love in that it is experienced in the presence of the beloved or when good comes to the beloved.[11] Thus, in relation to love, fear and joy become in a sense second cousins. But when fear becomes disordered, it relates to joy not as a relative but as an enemy. It casts a shadow over the presence of the beloved, as the possibility of future danger elbows aside present happiness. We find ourselves unable to rejoice in the presence of what we love because we are too afraid of losing it.

One day a lawyer approaches Jesus and asks him, "What must I do to inherit eternal life?" Jesus responds by reaffirming the Jewish teaching that we should love God and neighbor. The lawyer (being a lawyer) asks for further clarification. "Who is my neighbor?" He asks a question of contraction, a question of limits. Where does my responsibility end? Perhaps it is even a question of fear. Remember, the lawyer wants to know how to inherit eternal life. Perhaps he fears eternal death. And if the circle of love is too wide, it becomes all the more difficult to keep the command.

Jesus responds by telling a story about a man, beaten and robbed, left by the side of the road. A priest and a Levite pass by but refuse to bother themselves with the hurting man. A Samaritan, however, passes by and willingly extends himself to the stranger, giving assistance, time, and money. "Which of these three, do you think, was a neighbor to the man who fell into the hands of the robbers?" Jesus asks. "The one who showed him mercy," replies the lawyer. "Go and do likewise," says Jesus (Luke 10:25–37). Jesus refuses to confine our care and concern to a limited group. "Neighbor" is not a quality someone has to have in order to be cared for; rather, "neighbor" is a quality of those who show mercy to the broken. Such an extension of the heart cannot be achieved in a state of systolic fear, for we may find, as the Samaritan did, that the person in need is the very enemy we have been warned about.

## Faith's Daring

Over fifty years ago, Hans Urs von Balthasar wrote words that ring true today: "Only a Christian who does not allow himself to be infected by modern humanity's neurotic anxiety . . . has any hope of exercising a Christian influence on this age. He will not haughtily turn away from the anxiety of his fellow men and fellow Christians but will show them how to extricate themselves from their fruitless withdrawal into themselves and will point out the paths by which they can step out into the open, into faith's daring."[12] Faith must be daring, because following Jesus is risky; it may involve losing life in order to find it. The call of discipleship does not promise security; rather, in the words of Dietrich Bonhoeffer, a German theologian and martyr, "When Christ calls a man, he bids him come and die."[13]

I used to think that the angels in the Bible began their messages with "Do not be afraid" because their appearance was so frightening. But I suspect they began this way because the quieting of fear is required in order to hear and do what God asks of us. Fear makes it difficult to embrace the vulnerability involved in discipleship. Following Jesus requires that we step out "into faith's daring."

Theologian David Ford writes about the ways our lives are shaped by "overwhelmings."[14] Some of these are good, and some are bad. Ford notes that when we're dealing with overwhelming experiences, tinkering with small details is not so helpful—for instance, dealing with apocalyptic fears by storing a bin of canned food and duct tape in the basement.[15] Nor is it helpful simply to tell ourselves, "I should not be overwhelmed by this." We cannot command ourselves to feel less fear. Quite the contrary, our overwhelming fears need, themselves, to be overwhelmed by bigger and better things, by a sense of adventure and fullness of life that comes from locating our fears and vulnerabilities within a larger story that is ultimately hopeful and not tragic. Ford writes, "[Jesus] taught his disciples that there was no following the way of the kingdom of God without being willing to stake their life on it. . . . It is a basic instance of overwhelming: Abundance of life and immersion in death are inseparable."[16] Only by facing death, our most primal fear, can we move ahead to embrace life with the great "nevertheless" that is God's gracious word to a broken world.

## Fear and Shame

I realize that language of "putting fear in its place" evokes, perhaps, the image of forcefully cordoning off fear's perimeter. Or it might suggest deflating a puffed-up and overbearing fear, cutting it down to size. But each of these images conjures a forceful negation of something within ourselves, a negation that can feed the idea that we should be ashamed of our fear. The connection between shame and fear has been wisely explored by James Finley. He writes,

> So why are we so afraid of fear? We are afraid of fear because we believe that it has the power to name who we are, and it fills us with shame. We feel ashamed that we're going around as a fearful person, and so we pretend that we're not afraid. We try our best to find our own way out of feeling afraid, but this is our dilemma, our stuck place, that Jesus wants us to be liberated from. But we cannot do it on our own. . . . Jesus invites us to discover that our fear is woven into God's own

life, whose life is mysteriously woven into all the scary things that can and do happen to us as human beings together on this earth. This is liberation from fear in the midst of a fearful situation.[17]

Finley offers three helpful observations. First, we recoil not only from fearful things but from the fear we find in ourselves. And because we experience fear as weakness, we feel shame at our inability to stave it off. Second, we cannot get out of the stuck-ness of fear by ourselves. Third, Jesus invites us to see that "fear is woven into God's own life"—by which Finley means, I think, that even the things that threaten to undo us in this life are taken up and transformed by God. God's life is "woven into all the scary things" not in the sense that God is causing or desiring the scary things but that even in fear God can be found. And if God is there, then this is no shameful place that must be hidden.

We release the shame of fear when we acknowledge the fear that is in us. *To put fear in its place is also to give fear a place,* to appreciate the way fear seeks to protect us, and to recognize that *when fear has a place, it no longer needs to have every place.*

Richard Rohr makes the case that "everything belongs." God is in all things and all things are in God—there is no "outside" to be rejected, there is no "other" to be resisted. And if this is true, then fear, too, has a place. "The fears that assault us are mostly simple anxieties about social skills, about intimacy, about likeableness, or about performance. We need not give emotional food or charge to these fears or become attached to them. We don't even have to shame ourselves for having these fears. Simply ask your fears, 'What are you trying to teach me?'"[18] The more we resist fear head on, the more power it has over us. Our ability to bend with the pressures of fear allows it to slip past us, to nudge without controlling.

## QUESTIONS AND EXERCISES

So how do we give fear a place and put fear in its place? In place of the usual discussion questions, I want to end this chapter with some questions and exercises that a person or a community could use when they feel fear. Some of these draw on left-brain analysis to help us know if fear is a reasonable response to what is before us. Some of these draw on right-brain exploration to help us release the power that fear has to distort and contract our lives. They are intended to help us reflect on our fear rather than simply react to it.

- Is the thing you fear actually present or fast approaching? Or is it far off, either in terms of distance (like a tornado that is a hundred miles away), time (like something that won't likely happen for years), or likelihood (like something that happens to one out of a million people)?
- Is the thing you fear really a threat? That is, will it really cause you to lose something you love, or does it just seem scary because it is strange?
- Do you fear so much that you are closing in on yourself or unjustly lashing out at others?
- Does your fear take away the joy you feel in the presence of things you love (like family, friendships, or work) because you are afraid of losing them?
- Is your fear the result of someone's attempt to manipulate you? Is anyone profiting from your fearfulness (like a business getting your money, a politician getting your vote, or a religious leader getting your offering)?
- Does your fear keep you from doing things you know you should do?
- Try to welcome your fear long enough to become curious about it. Ask, "What are you trying to teach me?"

- Does your fear fill you with shame about your weakness? Are there people in your life with whom you can share your fear and shame so that it does not control you by its hiddenness?
- Spend some time with the "serenity prayer," which invites you to replace fear with acceptance, courage, and wisdom: "God, grant me the serenity to accept the things I cannot change, the courage to change the things I can, and the wisdom to know the difference."

# 5

# Community and Courage

If you have ever been home alone at night when you are used to having others in the house, you might have heard noises—squeaks and thumps—that you had never noticed before. The empty house feels more threatening even if there is no real reason to believe you are in danger. Simply being alone can make us feel vulnerable. Being alone can make it difficult to put danger and fear in perspective. Without the presence of others, living courageously can feel like a daunting task.

## Loneliness and Fear

The epidemic of loneliness and alienation in our culture adds to our fear, since our own resources often seem a meager stay against outside threats. As Frank Furedi notes, "Many people are literally on their own. Such social isolation enhances the sense of insecurity. Many of society's characteristic obsessions—with health, safety and security—are the products of this experience of social isolation."[1] Our culture of fear is also a culture of disconnection.

There is a particular genre of reality TV that has provided salient examples of isolation within artificial community. Shows such as *Survivor*, *The Apprentice*, *The Bachelor*, and *The Bachelorette* set contestants in a context of communal living in which the participants can work together insofar as it helps each individual defeat all the others. Thus, even as the contestants weep, rage, and bare their souls together, each lives in fear that they will be the next one sent home. Such shows reveal the anxiety produced by a culture that highly prizes individual achievement even as we yearn for communal connection.

Though many today speak of the virtues of community, the practical realities of our lives make real community uncommon. We are more mobile than ever, which means many of us live far from extended family. We participate in a competitive economy where the coworker is also the competition for the next promotion. We live in a time when traditions, narratives, and communities have largely lost their moral authority. We believe that our decisions should be our own, but this often cuts us off from the wisdom of others. When we cannot assume a shared social or moral vision, our isolation grows.

Furedi connects our obsession with individual freedom and our isolation: "Whether they like it or not, people have been 'freed' from many of the relations which linked individuals together in the past, so, in principle, people are free to choose their lifestyles and relations. But in the absence of new forms of social solidarities, such freedom helps to intensify the sense of estrangement and of powerlessness. It is as if people must 'choose,' whether they like it or not."[2]

Lacking networks of social support, we float in a sea of uncertainty. The absence of community—both the community of the dead that we call tradition and the community of the living—adds to our fear because it becomes less clear what it looks like to live well. And apart from some such definition, we remain anxious about our choices. The absence of community also leaves us with a sense that our resources are scarce, since we cannot necessarily count on the support of others in difficult times.

As a community, we can bear risks together that we might be reluctant to face alone. So if we are to recover courageous living, we need to recover the kind of community capable of supporting it. A community of religious brothers in Taizé, France, provides a remarkable witness to just such communal courage in a fearful world.

### Taizé: Courage in Community

The Taizé community was founded in 1940, when Brother Roger sought to create a sanctuary in southern France to assist refugees, Jews and non-Jews, during World War II. Over the years, Taizé has grown into an ecumenical monastic community of over a hundred brothers. No one who visits Taizé can fail to be moved by the bonds of solidarity that are created among the brothers and the thousands of people each year who make pilgrimage to this small French town.

I remember my first visit to Taizé in the summer of 1990. I took a youth group from my church, and we spent a week in prayer, song, reflection, and fellowship. We met other young pilgrims from all over the world. We knew almost immediately that our faith linked us in a way that broke down boundaries of race, tribe, and nation. A large group from Poland had arrived just before we did, so during that week the community often sang in Polish—a difficult language for English speakers to read. We quickly gave up trying to decipher the words on the page and began to learn the songs by ear, letting ourselves settle into the repetitive rhythms. Soon we were singing along, not always sure what we were saying, but knowing that we were united with our brothers and sisters through Christ in a kind of Pentecost moment.

Being a community of reconciliation, where moments such as these happen day after day, week after week, constitutes the central mission of the brothers. When a new brother makes a lifelong commitment to the community, the service includes the words, "The Lord Christ . . . has chosen you to be in the Church a sign of brotherly love. It is his will that with your brothers you live the parable of community."[3] This metaphor, "parable of community," has become one of the most prominent self-descriptions of Taizé.

Alongside "parable of community," one often hears Taizé characterized as a "pilgrimage of trust on earth," a description given by Brother Roger. This has become the theme of yearly gatherings around the globe, which bring together tens of thousands of people, mostly young adults, to pray, contemplate, converse, and embrace Brother Roger's vision of trust. Community and trust, two things that are often missing in today's world, define Taizé. We learn to trust as we learn to embrace community. The support of the larger body helps us become people who can risk enough to trust.

This trust was threatened when tragedy struck the community during a prayer service on Tuesday, August 16, 2005. As the worshipers sang and the brothers knelt, a woman emerged from the congregation with a knife and murdered the ninety-year-old Brother Roger in his wheelchair. The community was shocked and grieved, as were all those who had become friends of Taizé over the years. The brothers were left to respond to this violence and to reflect on how it would affect the life and mission of the community. How could they sustain their mission when the trust they preached had been broken in the most violent way imaginable?

Otto Selles, a professor in the French department at Calvin College, tells of his experience with the brothers a few months after the attack. Selles had planned to bring nineteen students from Calvin to Taizé during the fall term following the attack. Upon hearing the news, he became concerned that this event might change Taizé, creating an atmosphere of fear and suspicion.

> Would the community's spirit be broken? And practically, would Taizé restrict access to the Brothers? "Nothing at Taizé has changed. There is no security," said Brother Jean-Marie, when my group finally arrived in lower Burgundy for a very chilly November weekend retreat at Taizé. . . . And while the community continues to grieve Brother Roger's death, he stressed that "the community is very, very united." . . . After the visit, I realized why the Brothers would probably never put metal detectors in the Church of Reconciliation—their sense of spiritual security and calm goes miles deeper than most of us would like to admit.[4]

In our anxious times, we need all the more to attend to that parable of community. Like the parables of Jesus, this fellowship of brothers functions to subvert our easy expectations about how the world works. Just as the surprising grace of the father stuns us in the parable of the prodigal son, just as the imprudent generosity of the employer shocks us in the parable of the workers in the vineyard, so the simple resumption of a life of community and trust surprises us in the lived parable of Taizé. "There is no security," says Brother Jean-Marie. No security? After the founder of the community had been stabbed to death by a woman who carried in a knife for this very purpose, one could imagine making a very good case for metal detectors. Surely some process of screening the visitors would be sensible? But parables do not exist to reinforce our assumptions about caution and common sense. They put us face-to-face with God's profound grace and urge us to take the risk of loving others as God does.

## Courage and Violence

In the face of a deadly attack, it is easy to imagine a violent response to be necessary and even courageous in order to protect oneself and others. Aristotle elevated the soldier as the paradigm of courage, and it is no wonder, since in Athens the warrior was the primary example of one who puts self-interest and self-protection aside for the good of the city. But as Christian theologians began to read Aristotle, this conviction was challenged. In a tradition that looks to Jesus as the paradigm of all human virtue, it is a hard stretch to see armed warfare as the exemplary embodiment of courageous action.

In his discussion of courage (or "fortitude"), Aquinas argues that "the principal act of fortitude is endurance, that is to stand immovable in the midst of dangers rather than to attack them. Endurance is more difficult that aggression."[5] While fear naturally (and properly) moderates our tendency to become rash or inordinately daring, courage is needed to moderate fear, which is our tendency to retreat or contract. Real courage is shown primarily in our ability to endure, to stand with fortitude, rather than in our willingness to attack. In contrast to Aristotle, Aquinas defines martyrdom as the paradigm case of Christian courage—endurance rather than aggression.

Writing in the early days of the Cold War, Hans Urs von Balthasar wrestled with a similar question and came to a similar conclusion. He writes,

> Consider the abysmal problem of the relation between God's Kingdom and earthly power . . . : whether, for example, a call to arms by the Church, a blessing of weapons, or taking up the sword of this world is an expression of the courage of Christian faith, or, on the contrary, the symptom of an unchristian and faithless anxiety; whether something that can be defended and justified in a hundred ways with penultimate reasons drawn from faith . . . will collapse miserably before

the throne of judgment of the *ultimate* reason—because what of course appeared to be God's weapon in the hands of God's warrior against God's enemies is now suddenly exposed as Peter's desperate sword-waving against the high priest's servant, whose side Jesus takes in order to expose such brandishing of weapons for what it was: anxious betrayal. To be a Christian in the church requires courage.[6]

Neither Aquinas nor Balthasar was a pacifist. But each knew that if one is a Christian, one begins with a presumption against violence. The paradigm of courage is not the soldier but the martyr.

## Courage and Recklessness

Courage is the capacity to do what is right and good in the face of fear. We become courageous when we learn to live for something that is more important than our own safety. The Taizé community exists not to preserve itself but to give the world a taste of God's kingdom. For them, courage takes the form of living their life of hospitality and reconciliation even when they feel threatened. Jesus showed courage when "he set his face to go to Jerusalem" (Luke 9:51), knowing that he was walking into a religious and political powder keg. He knew that his mission was more important than his safety.

We might want to ask how we know that the actions of the Taizé community or the boldness of Jesus is "courageous" and not just reckless. If you know that you are a marked man, do you walk straight into a crowded public place and announce yourself by raising a ruckus in the temple? If you have been attacked, do you continue with business as usual? How do we discern the difference between courage and foolishness?

First, having courage does not mean that you lack fear or that you ignore your fear. As Aristotle notes, a person would have to be "a sort of madman or insensible person if he feared nothing" (remember the Brothers Grimm fable). Aristotle goes on, "The man who exceeds in confidence about what really is terrible is rash. The rash man, however, is also thought to be boastful and only a pretender to courage."[7] Feeling no fear at all would make one a "madman," while being excessively confident in the face of fear makes one rash. Neither of these is to be confused with courage. The courageous person feels fear but is not overcome by it. The courageous person recognizes danger but refuses to let fear get in the way of doing what is right, good, and necessary. The courageous person also shows prudence in the face of danger, since prudence (or "practical wisdom") is an important companion virtue to courage. Prudence rightly tells us that there is no virtue in taking the wrong kind of risks. Prudence helps us discern the difference between being rash and having courage.

Not all risky behavior is courageous, even when it is intended for good. There are some risks that we need not take, since our own lives are gifts from God, and faithfulness calls us to value those gifts. A Christian community can provide a place to weigh judgments about courageous action. The community ought to be a place of discernment, so that we do not need to rely on individual judgments alone.

## Community and Courage

How do we learn to be courageous? We learn courage pretty much the way we learn everything else—by watching other people. And if "friendship is the crucible of the moral life,"[8] then the virtues we need to live well are shaped by sharing a life together with friends who help us become good. Virtues are learned by being with others who embody the virtues. A virtue is different from a rule or a principle, for as with a musical score, you cannot really know what a virtue is like on paper—it has to be performed. We learn to be virtuous by seeing virtuous people act in virtuous ways.

Anglican theologian John Milbank argues that "virtue cannot properly operate except when collectively possessed."[9] This is never truer than when talking about courage. Courage requires community, both for the learning of courage and the living of it. And this community is not just of the present but of all those who have gone before us. In the reading of Scripture and the remembrance of the saints, we recall all those who have embodied courage in the past, and we pray for the strength to imitate them.

As Aquinas indicated, the martyrs are especially important, since they embody the most powerful witness to courage we can imagine. They recognize that discipleship requires risk, but they do not step back from it. They live for something bigger than self-preservation, so the threat of death does not scare them into unfaithfulness. They are sustained by communities that not only teach them courage but also promise to tell their stories to future generations. The courage of the martyr relies upon the courage of a community that dares to keep the martyr's story alive. Today more than ever, our churches need to be telling and celebrating these stories.

It is possible, conversely, that a Christian community's life will work against courage. Over time a church can settle into patterns that turn the focus inward and tempt a people to become content with self-preservation. Some have called such communities "maintenance churches"[10] because they seem to have little sense of mission beyond keeping the doors open. There is no courageous reaching out, there is no bold risking of time or resources. Rather, there is careful consideration of how to preserve the good thing they've got going. Such churches, while they may offer a great deal to those who attend, could hardly be considered courageous and would be unlikely places for individuals to develop the virtue of courage.

## Giving Words to Fear

Developing courage requires not only a community that embodies courage but a community in which our fears can be given voice. Too often even church can be a place where we feel the need to hide our fears, to "dress up" so that we become presentable to God and others. This usually requires hiding the dark stuff underneath a smile and a handshake. Church can, unfortunately, be a place where vulnerability is met with either judgment or platitudes. Yet fear grows all the more powerful when we cannot speak it. To give words to our fear, to name our fear, is to begin to dispel its power.

Yann Martel explores this theme in his novel *Life of Pi*. The main character, Piscine Patel, known as Pi, lives in Pondicherry, India, with a literary mother and a rationalist father. To the chagrin of both his parents, Pi seems to be inescapably religious (he practices Christianity, Islam, and Hinduism all at the same time). Pi's father runs the zoo in Pondicherry, until the money dries up and he decides to move. The family and some of the remaining zoo animals board a Japanese ship headed to Canada, but on the way the ship sinks. The only survivors are Pi and a 450-pound Bengal tiger named Richard Parker. For 227 days they drift through a series of adventures, real and imagined, hoping for shore or rescue. While on the boat Pi begins to reflect on his fears (alternately the fear of dying at sea and the fear of being eaten by Richard Parker).

> I must say a word about fear. It is life's only true opponent. Only fear can defeat life. It is a clever, treacherous adversary, how well I know. It has no decency, respects no law or convention, shows no mercy. It goes for your weakest spot, which it finds with unerring ease. It begins in your mind, always. One moment you are feeling calm, self-possessed, happy. Then fear, disguised in the garb of mild-mannered doubt, slips into your mind like a spy. Doubt meets disbelief and disbelief tries to push it out. But

disbelief is a poorly armed foot soldier. Doubt does away with
it with little trouble. You become anxious. Reason comes to do
battle for you. You are reassured. Reason is fully equipped with
the latest weapons technology. But, to your amazement, despite
superior tactics and a number of undeniable victories, reason is
laid low. You feel yourself weakening, wavering. Your anxiety
becomes dread. Quickly you make rash decisions. You dismiss
your last allies: hope and trust. There, you've defeated yourself.
Fear, which is but an impression, has triumphed over you.[11]

Neither disbelief nor reason, two skills Pi's parents have tried
to teach him, can win a battle with fear. His judgment that fear
is "but an impression" echoes Aquinas's description of fear as
an act of the imagination. Yet locating fear in the imagination
does not make it any less real. It only highlights its specter-like
quality, its ability to evade the grasp that would subdue it. Once
disbelief and reason fail to fend off fear, one makes the rash
decision to dismiss hope and trust. These are, according to Pi,
one's "last allies." But how can one avoid that rash decision,
that pit-of-the-stomach sense of inevitability that causes a person to lose hope and give up trust? By putting fear into words.

Fear, Pi continues, "seeks to rot everything, even the words
with which to speak of it." Therefore, "you must fight hard to
shine the light of words upon it. Because if you don't, if your
fear becomes a wordless darkness that you avoid, perhaps even
manage to forget, you open yourself to further attacks of fear because you never truly fought the opponent who defeated you."[12]
Words make it possible to share fear. To speak our fear to another
is to begin to loosen the grip that fear has on us. To make fear
take form in speech is to name it as something that can be confronted—not confronted alone but in the community of those
willing to speak their fears aloud and thus begin to subdue them.

In her Nobel lecture, Toni Morrison weaves a story of a
woman, "blind but wise," the daughter of slaves, who is known

for her clairvoyance. This woman is visited by children bent on tricking her, "showing her up for the fraud they believe she is."[13] But as they talk with her and begin to see her wisdom, they plead,

> Make up a story. Narrative is radical, creating us at the very moment it is being created. We will not blame you if your reach exceeds your grasp; if love so ignites your words they go down in flames and nothing is left but their scald. Or if, with the reticence of a surgeon's hands, your words suture only the places where blood might flow. We know you can never do it properly—once and for all. Passion is never enough; neither is skill. But try. For our sake and yours forget your name in the street; tell us what the world has been to you in the dark places and in the light. Don't tell us what to believe, what to fear. Show us belief's wide skirt and the stitch that unravels fear's caul. . . . Language alone protects us from the scariness of things with no names.[14]

The children's supplication for a story to protect them "from the scariness of things with no names" echoes Pi's plea to "fight hard to shine the light of words upon" our fears. Stories told can "unravel fear's caul."

At its best, the church is a place where such stories are told. In baptism we tell the story of how Jesus faced death, our fundamental fear, so that we—like him—might overcome it. We confess our sins, daring to name "things we have done and things we have left undone." And so we become a gathering in which fears and failings can be expressed honestly since we no longer believe they control us.

The church needs to become a place where we are not ashamed to hear the fears of others or to share our own. It needs to become a place that helps us find the words to bring fear out of the "wordless darkness." This may happen through small groups and support groups where we come to trust one another well enough to be vulnerable. It may happen through the liturgy, especially the psalms of lament, which allow us to voice our fears and anxieties. It may happen in the sermon, as preachers name from the pulpit the fears that grip us. And when it does happen, we will begin to become communities of courage precisely because we have found ways to name, and thus confront, the fears that keep us from living fully and joyfully.

## Sharing Risks and Resources

Some might respond that words can only go so far, for without resources to defend against real threats, our words will be empty. And there is some truth to this. Having courage requires a community not just where fear can be spoken but where risks and resources can be shared. Jesus models a life in which resources are relinquished. Jesus challenges our attempts to find security in wealth or power. He deflates the ambitions of those disciples who, after the Last Supper, argue over who will hold the highest position in Jesus's administration. He says to them, "the greatest among you must become like the youngest, and the leader like one who serves" (Luke 22:25–26). Jesus redefines power and relativizes riches. He makes our lives potentially more dangerous and thus more fearful. Yet he also calls his followers into a shared life in which no one has to have all the resources to meet threats and dangers, since the resources of the community are at the disposal of anyone in need. What is lost in terms of goods accumulated for one's security is gained back in a network of shared risks and resources.

This strikes me as the real point of the communal sharing described in Acts. Early Christians interpreted Jesus's call to relinquish wealth not as a demand for absolute poverty, but as a decision to open all of their resources to the needs of others. So, rather than becoming poorer, everyone became richer. Though Acts may at times idealize the early church, it gives us a vision of shared risks and resources that could be very helpful for overcoming fear. If I really believed that if I lost my job or my child got sick, I would not have to respond on my own, then I might fear the future less. If I really believed that the resources of my community were open to me in case of an emergency, then I might fear the emergency less. If I really believed that my community would support my family if I got arrested protesting for peace, then I might be more likely to summon the courage and take a stand.

Paul Wadell observes that "it is much easier to take the risk of loving someone when we know we are loved and cherished by another."[15] The presence of a loving community makes it easier to take the risk of extending love to someone outside the community. Here we come back to the connection of hospitality and courage with which we began the chapter. The brothers of Taizé are able to take the risk of loving and welcoming the stranger, even the potentially dangerous stranger, because they share a common life in which their common love supports the extension of that love. There can be no solution to fear without communities that can bear fear together.

## QUESTIONS FOR DISCUSSION

1. What is your response to the decision of the Taizé brothers not to put any security in place after the murder of Brother Roger? Does it strike you as irresponsible? Courageous? Both?

2. Think of a time when someone's courage impressed you. What made the act courageous and not just reckless?

3. How have you seen isolation contribute to fear in your life or those around you? What do you think it will take to restore community in the church and beyond?

4. This chapter uses *Life of Pi* to help us think about fear. Can you think of other stories, novels, or movies that give insights into fear or courage?

5. Have you heard of or been a part of a church in which the members actually offered tangible support (goods and money) to one another as needed? Do you think it could happen? What would it take?

# 6

# Trust and Hope

Let's be honest. These days hope is hard to come by, and trust feels like a luxury we can't afford. The people we think we can trust too often disappoint us. We are all too aware of how duplicitous people can be. The #MeToo movement has pulled back the curtain on untrustworthy men who exploit positions of power. The #BlackLivesMatter movement has exposed a criminal justice system that routinely fails people of color. As trust is lost, it is hard to hang on to hope. We can only hope *for* something when we can trust *in* something. Theologically speaking, we have hope for better days because we trust in God, who holds the future. Without hope there is no alternative to fear, and without trust there is no hope.

Remember Pi Patel out on the boat in the ocean? Hope and trust, he tells us, are our "last allies" against fear. Courage alone cannot be sustained without some hope that things can get better. So, how do we rebuild hope and trust when dreams being dashed seems much more likely than dreams coming true? We need a story that gives us something to hope for, that not only tells the truth about hope deferred but also gives us reason to trust that the future can be different from the past. While the whole biblical narrative provides something like this for Christians, the distinctive lineaments of that story emerge clearly when we compare the two pivotal gardens in the Bible—the garden of Eden and the garden of Gethsemane.

These two gardens reflect each other as mirror images. In Eden, the first Adam sins through disobedience and pride; in Gethsemane, the second Adam redeems the world from sin through obedience and humility. In the first garden humankind falls and receives a curse; in the second garden humankind is redeemed and receives blessing. The tree in the first story that occasions sin is replaced by the tree in the second upon which Christ dies for sin. But one of the most interesting parallels is that in the first garden, humankind knows fear for the first time and hides from God. In the second, Jesus knows fear for the first time and remains faithful to God. Each knows fear, but they offer us alternative paths for responding to that fear— trust or suspicion, hope or despair. To unpack these alternatives, we will start this chapter in the first garden and end in the second.

### Trust in Eden: Blessing

The creation stories of Genesis describe human beings as made for blessing. As Kendall Soulen puts it, God's blessing communicates "life, wholeness, well-being, and joy."[1] Blessings are received as gifts from God but are then passed on between people and within creation in an ongoing exchange of gifts, a kind of heavenly economy on earth. And blessing requires two things: difference (because you don't need to receive what you already have) and mutual dependence (because we have to rely on each other).[2]

In Genesis 12 the natural economy of blessing is supplemented by a political economy of blessing—Abram and Sarai are chosen to parent a nation, a people who will be blessed and who will be a blessing to others. The gifts of blessing are given in order to be passed on, in order to flow through God's people and beyond them. The logic of blessing is not to pay it back but to pay it forward. Israel is to pay forward to the nations what they have received from God.

Blessing includes not only material things that sustain well-being but the rhythms of time that organize labor and leisure. The blessing of the Sabbath day invites us to rest, to enter the slow rhythm of divine gift, to practice waiting, patience, and receptivity. A frenetic posture toward time—the fear that there is not enough time—defeats blessing, because it turns us into those who grasp and hoard rather than those who receive and release. With the giving of blessing comes the expectation that it will be passed on, especially to those who in conventional terms have not earned it. Blessing is sustained by trust that as goods are released they are not lost. Blessing is sustained by hope that what has once been offered will be received again.

## Losing Trust in Eden: Fear

But fear enters the biblical story very early, and it becomes a threat to blessing. Fear says there is not enough to go around. Fear says there is not enough to be generous. Fear says grasp and hold on to what you can get. Ironically, or perhaps all too predictably, this fear produces the very scarcity it is afraid of.

In Genesis 3, Adam and Eve eat the fruit of the forbidden tree and become afraid for the first time. They hide from each other and cover their naked bodies with leaves. Why do they do this? Shame? Embarrassment? Perhaps. But I think something more is behind this hiding. Having transgressed the boundaries of God, they feel that the boundaries of their own bodies are no longer secure; they cannot trust their vulnerability with each other; they fear each other and they hide from each other. Blessing becomes blocked by fear.

Simone Weil gives a fascinating reading of this story, seeing it as an attempt to consume beauty. She writes, "It may be that vice, depravity, and crime are nearly always, or even perhaps always, in their essence, attempts to eat beauty, to eat what we should only look at." So, if Adam and Eve "caused humanity to be lost by eating the fruit, the opposite attitude, looking at the fruit without eating it, should be what is required to save it."[3] Weil's interpretation helps us understand why human beings fear each other. The beautiful is meant to be gazed upon, to be delighted in, not to be plucked and consumed. A proper response to blessing allows the beauty of another—another person, another object—to exist outside of oneself in such a way that its integrity is maintained and its gifts can be extended. But the first humans cannot trust abundance, and lacking trust, they give in to fear.

As the story continues, so do the themes of fear and hiding. The human beings hear the sound of God walking in the garden, and they hide among the trees. "Where are you?" calls God. Adam replies, "I heard the sound of you in the garden, and I was afraid, because I was naked; and I hid myself" (Gen. 3:9–10). Adam and Eve hide from God, but really they are hiding from death. Earlier in the story, God promised that if they ate of the forbidden fruit, they would die. God's presence suggests that this consequence is near. And so, both Adam and Eve seek to deflect the punishment, each offering up another to be sacrificed, to bear the penalty of death—"it was her fault," Adam says; "it was the serpent's fault," Eve says.

God responds to these attempts to deflect death onto the other by pronouncing a curse on all three of the creatures. For the woman and man, the curse strikes at the point where they should share the mutuality of blessing—bringing forth children and bringing forth food from the earth. Those who would sacrifice another for their own security are now fated to struggle for goods, and those things that should have come as blessing—offspring and sustenance—are now brought forth in pain. Curse is the reversal, the dark underside, of the blessing for which humankind was created.

This story in the garden reveals the common elements of all our fears, for they return in one way or another to the fear of death, the fear of the other, and our willingness to sacrifice others to make ourselves safe. As the biblical story moves forward, it is disordered fear, as much as anything, that keeps us trapped in sin and curse. And as self-preservation becomes the highest good, we find ourselves unwilling to risk sharing God's blessing with one another and all the more willing to destroy potential threats to our safety. The inability to trust in God's abundance leaves humans trapped in fear. This fear, in turn, traps blessing in an unending parody of gift in which goods remain safely managed in a circle of exchange between those who "have," leaving those who "have not" outside the flow of blessing. Short of trusting in God's provision, we have a hard time getting over the fear that the flow of gift might not flow back to us. After Eden, trust and hope are in short supply.

## Cynicism and Irony

Trust and hope can be overwhelmed by fear, but they can also be subverted by cynicism and irony—fear's bedfellows. And that shouldn't surprise us. Once we come to believe we can't trust each other, then we treat each other as untrustworthy. So begins a cycle of self-fulfilling prophecy. When we find ourselves in a culture that is shot through with abuses of power and a political system that reeks of self-interest, we are halfway to despair. But along the way we pause long enough to try on cynicism and irony. If cynicism is the offspring of disillusionment, irony is the aftermath of betrayal. Cynicism plays at realism but ends up being a strategy for evading responsibility. Irony pretends at sincerity then turns and laughs at those who believed us. We want to avoid appearing naïve or sentimental. We want to have an escape hatch so that when our desire goes unfulfilled we can tell ourselves (and others) that we never really wanted it in the first place. When hope and trust fail, we look for whatever cover we can find.

I have to say, I have a lot of sympathy for the doubting Thomases of our day. For academics, cynicism is an occupational hazard. We are rewarded for taking the high road, and by that I don't mean a *moral* high road. I mean a posture of detachment that gazes from an analytical perch down on the projects of others. While this analytical height can sometimes aid in research, it can be bad for the soul. It is easy to believe that we are wiser than the practitioners of the things we are studying. The religion professor who teaches and writes about religion all week does not easily set aside the evaluative posture in order to become an unselfconscious worshiper.

Martha Nussbaum reminds us that the ancients ran into this very same problem. "Stoicism and cynicism are perennial threats for the hopeful. The cynic scoffs at the romantic dreams of hopers. The stoic is less openly hostile but shrinks back from the waters of life into an insular detachment."[4] Stoicism, cynicism, irony, and detachment all look like good options in a time when many feel disappointed, betrayed, and hopeless. But to give in to despair is to dismiss our last allies. In our attempt to avoid hurt and disappointment, we give up the very things we need to keep fear from defeating us.

The protective moat of detachment keeps us from taking the risks necessary to find joy. Hope and trust ask us to go all in, which means we have a lot to lose. In a way, we have to trust already in order to begin to trust. It could be a vicious circle unless someone takes the risk of trusting first.

## Reclaiming Hope

The prophet Jeremiah, speaking to an Israel that had been defeated and sent into exile, wrote, "For surely I know the plans I have for you, says the LORD, plans for your welfare and not for harm, to give you a future with hope" (Jer. 29:11). Our ability to live in trust and hope rests on our ability imagine such a future. Fear and hope are essentially acts of the imagination. Each disposition imagines a future—one bad, one good—that orients a person's actions in the present. We experience fear when we look to the future and imagine hurt, sorrow, or loss that is going to be hard to avoid. We experience hope when we look to the future and imagine joy, pleasure, or gain that is going to be hard to attain. Both fear and hope are characterized by the expectation of future struggle—against future harms or against the obstacles to happiness. Hope and fear parallel each other in the same way as good and evil, hate and love, desire and aversion.

Whether one looks toward the future with fear or hope goes a long way toward determining one's fundamental attitude and actions. Do we imagine the future primarily in terms of the goods it may bring to us or in terms of the evils we hope to avoid? While we may all feel some fear and some hope when looking ahead, one of the two will prove more determinative of our actions; one of the two will provide our principal orientation toward the future. If, on the one hand, it is fear, then we will all too quickly arm ourselves for battle or collapse into a mode of self-preservation. We may hear Jesus promising that "those who lose their life for my sake will find it" (Matt. 10:39), but we are too afraid to take the risks involved in losing ourselves. If, on the other hand, our orientation toward the future is hope, we will find ourselves able to embrace life and to risk radical discipleship (perhaps even to "lose ourselves") because we trust that the future is ultimately in God's hands.

All that said, we have to be careful about hope because, as Barbara Brown Taylor observes, "Christian hope can become an excuse for checking out of the present, especially when the fulfillment of that hope rests solely in God's hands."[5] She goes on, "My Anglicanism may be showing here, but I do trust that God not only invites human participation in the healing of the world but also insists on it, to the point that God refuses to act alone."[6] She sends up an important warning flare. Hope in God can become an excuse to avoid human responsibility (oddly enough, not unlike cynicism). It can instill passivity when what is needed is urgency. "I pray not for hope in the future but for trust in the present," she writes. "That way I am never tempted to go to sleep for a hundred years and hope that everything is better when I wake up."[7] Point taken. But perhaps trust in the present and hope for the future can go hand in hand.

We might hear in Taylor's caution a distinction between what has been called "idle hope" and "practical hope."[8] One removes our sense of agency and urgency, the other "energizes a commitment to action."[9] At its best, hope does not undermine responsibility but instead undergirds and inspires transformative work because we are saved from the despairing lie that our actions cannot make a difference.

## Relationship as a Source of Trust

One example of such hope-filled work is The People's Supper, an organization that uses shared meals to help people from different backgrounds, identities, and beliefs come together to build connection and trust. In partnership with other organizations—schools, businesses, faith communities—they plan and carry out dinners "in order to strengthen our individual and collective resilience, and to repair the breach in our interpersonal relationships across political, ideological, and identity differences."[10]

Jennifer Bailey, cofounder of The People's Supper and a minister in the African Methodist Episcopal Church, tells the story of how her own experience of fear led to the work she is doing. On November 8, 2016—as the returns came in from the presidential election—Bailey found herself in tears, rocking back and forth on her kitchen floor. When she finally found words, she said, "I don't feel safe. I don't feel safe." At that moment, she sensed the presence of her mother, who had passed away earlier that year, saying to her, "We've never been safe." Reflecting on that experience, Bailey concludes, "It was a reminder for me . . . that safety is an illusion that's only afforded to a few people."[11]

One could easily imagine Bailey retreating into fight, flight, or freeze mode. But instead, she partnered with Lennon Flowers to create The People's Supper. One of the mantras of the project is, "Social change moves at the speed of relationships. Relationships move at the speed of trust." In an interview Bailey said, "There's been no movement for justice or equity in this country that didn't start with relationship. . . . And so, as I think about this work of social change that we're undertaking, the transformative practice of trying to build the America that we want to see, it's a generational project. And thank God that I believe in a faith tradition [in which] my time currency is eternity. It's not election cycles."[12] Bailey has an eternal horizon of hope, and yet this does not slow down her action in the present. Far from it. Her small-scale, transformative, dinner-table ministry only makes sense if there is a long arc of transformation and a reason to believe such efforts can succeed. Long-term hope for the future combined with trust building in the present creates a path beyond fear and suspicion.

The People's Supper imagines a space of blessing in which understanding is given and received, in which the reciprocity of shared food around the table meets the reciprocity of shared stories. The shape of the event pushes back against the fainthearted fear that would make us stingy with our blessing. There is a faint echo here of Jesus's injunction not to invite your relatives and friends to dinner, because they will just turn around and directly repay the gift with their own invitation. Rather, he says, cast the net of invitation wide: invite those who are not like you and those who cannot repay you, "and you will be blessed" (Luke 14:12–14).

If social change can only move as fast as relationships of trust are built, then we had better get to work. Hope for social change on the big scale requires the building of trust on the small scale. But too much fear can derail both projects.

## Trust in Gethsemane: Hope in Fear

So far we have found that (1) hope and trust are under threat by the betrayals of the powerful; (2) God creates us for blessing, which requires us to trust one another to reciprocate gifts; (3) our desire to grasp instead of gift results in fear and mistrust; (4) cynicism and irony are protective strategies for avoiding dashed hopes; (5) hope is an act of the imagination that, at its best, spurs transformative action; and (6) action toward a hopeful future moves only as fast as trust can be rebuilt.

At this point, I want to return to the biblical narrative with which we began the chapter. Eden shows us human beings caught in a web of fear and unable to trust one another or God long enough to discover the blessings of paradise. Gethsemane shows us Jesus agonizing with fear yet trusting God long enough to redeem the fallen choices of humanity. Unlike the newly minted humans in Genesis 3, Jesus neither hides from God nor offers up another to save himself. He moves toward God in his fear; he seeks relief, but his prayer is not "Save me at any cost." Rather, his prayer is "Your will be done."

100

This prayer reflects radical hope and radical trust. He does not presume to know exactly how God is going to deliver him, but he is quite sure that he will not be delivered through the active mistrust that leads to violence. Here in the garden, especially here, Jesus lives out his own command: "Love your enemies, do good to those who hate you, bless those who curse you" (Luke 6:27–28). He continues to participate in the economy of blessing even though his own life is threatened by those who are consumed with fear. When Peter seeks to defend Jesus with a preemptive strike, Jesus rebukes him and heals the slave who was wounded (22:50–51). Jesus refuses to allow fear to keep him from doing good. He goes to the cross in an act that extends blessing in the face of fear, and he pronounces forgiveness upon those who put him to death. Jesus's hope for a good ending to his story does not rest on his ability to control the outcome. It rests on his trust that the arc of God's story extends beyond the threatening events that are before him.

As he hangs on the cross, the chief priests, scribes, and elders mock him, saying, "He trusts in God; let God deliver him now" (Matt. 27:43). Though they use these words as a taunt, they are speaking truth. Yet a mere three verses later Jesus cries out, "My God, my God, why have you forsaken me?" (v. 46), making us wonder how much trust is left. Trust and hope fade far into the background in this moment. Jesus's hope is not certainty or presumption, but even in these words of resignation on the cross, his previous words of trust echo, "Not what I want but what you want" (26:39).

Jesus trusts himself to God's hands and to God's capacity to bring good from all things. He displays a response to fear that is paradigmatic in its opposition to the fearful failings of Eden. In Gethsemane and on the cross, Jesus shows what it looks like to trust in God's future while participating in God's present.

If the story ended here, we might respect the fortitude of Jesus. We might be amazed at his capacity to love when the rest of us would likely lash out in fear. We might see in him a tragic figure who shows the beautiful impossibility of overcoming the world's patterns of mistrust and curse. And that's not nothing. But the story doesn't end here. The resurrection vindicates Jesus's trust in God and opens up our own hope that death is not the final word.

Hope in the resurrection is quite different from hope in our ability to fend off death as long as possible. On this note, Rowan Williams does not mince words: "If your hope is that this life will be protected and prolonged, that your comfort zone as you understand it will never be challenged, that you will never have to face the reality of being mortal and limited, God help you. It's a recipe for illusion, terror and the killing of the soul."[13] Jesus's resurrection does not prove simply that in some general way death can be overcome. "What it proves is that God keeps his promises: the commitment of God the Father to Jesus his beloved son is absolute and eternal; . . . Jesus' life is there for [the disciples] once more, the source of their joy and hope. The violent and terrible death of Jesus does not stop God from giving what he wants to give, giving consistently and steadily. If Jesus is raised, we can count on the faithfulness of God."[14]

The hope of resurrection is not simply that beyond the grave we will find healing and completion, but that on this side of the grave we can trust God's promises. The resurrection of Jesus is a fulfillment of divine faithfulness. If we can trust God to be with and for us now, we can hope in a future that has been entrusted to God's hands. Living in trust and hope does not mean denying what is wrong with the world. It simply means that we can engage in work that points to a hopeful future even if that future, as Paul describes it, is seen only in a mirror dimly (1 Cor. 13:12).

## QUESTIONS FOR DISCUSSION

1. What makes it hard for you to have hope?

2. What makes it hard for you to trust?

3. Are there cultural and political forces that work against hope and trust? How would you describe them?

4. What gives you hope? Are there people or projects or movements that inspire you?

5. If you were to hold a People's Supper in your local setting, who would you want to be present at the table?

# 7

# Narrative and Providence

One way Christian communities have held on to hope and trust is through telling stories of God's provision—like the time God provided a ram for Abraham to sacrifice instead of Isaac, or provided manna in the desert to sustain the Israelites on their journey, or provided the Holy Spirit to a fearful group of disciples on Pentecost. In theological terms, we call this pattern of divine provision "providence." Providence is our ongoing affirmation of Abraham's words on Mount Moriah: "the LORD will provide" (Gen. 22:14). But many of us today find it more difficult to trust in God's providence than did those who lived in earlier times.

From the ancient church through the Reformation, Christians encountering danger or threat would have drawn strength from the belief that no matter what happened, God is the Lord of history. God's will could be seen in all that happened, even if seen only darkly. John Calvin provides a telling example of the premodern view that God controls all events. For Calvin this conviction produced a comfort that came from knowing that everything was in God's hands. He wrote,

> Innumerable are the evils that beset human life: innumerable, too, the deaths that threaten it. . . . Now, wherever you turn, all things around you not only are hardly to be trusted but almost openly menace, and seem to threaten immediate death. Embark upon a ship, you are one step away from death. Mount a horse, if one foot slips, your life is imperiled. Go through the city streets, you are subject to as many dangers as there are tiles on the roofs. . . . Amid these tribulations must not man be most miserable, since, but half alive in life, he weakly draws his anxious and languid breath, as if he had a sword perpetually hanging over his neck?[1]

Calvin gives us a glimpse of a sixteenth-century version of the culture of fear. Yet in the midst of his capacity to imagine future evils, Calvin found peace, because he believed that nothing would happen apart from God's will. Thus, he follows the previous litany of dangers with this affirmation: "Yet, when that light of divine providence has once shone upon a godly man, he is then relieved and set free not only from the extreme anxiety and fear that were pressing him before, but from every care."[2] Divine providence was, for Calvin, the affirmation that all things, big and small, flow from the will of God and therefore serve God's good purposes. The affirmation that God acts in the world to sustain, accompany, and guide the creation provided for premodern Christians a foundation for life.

And yet such a conviction as Calvin's brought with it a host of theological difficulties. Note that for Calvin we are set free from anxiety and fear not because we believe God will protect us from all danger but because we know that all that happens reflects God's will and serves God's plan. The shipwreck, the stumbling horse, the falling roof tiles that take frail human life are each the will of God, sometimes described as God's hidden will that cannot be understood by human minds. However, the sufferings and horrors of the modern era, along with the rise of scientific explanations for various natural and historical events, have made such a conviction either untenable or unnecessary for many Christians. What kind of God would will (hidden or otherwise) the kind of destruction wrought by the Holocaust, the World Wars, and the atomic bomb? While Calvin managed to draw comfort from his belief in a God who controls all things, few of us today find such a belief comforting. We are more likely to be repulsed by it. How did things change?

## The Loss of Providence

The demise of the doctrine of providence followed the arrival of alternative ways to narrate the accidents of nature and the events of history. During the seventeenth and eighteenth centuries, modern science and historical studies gave us purely natural explanations of the world, so appeals to God to make sense of things no longer seemed necessary. At the same time, traditional religious authorities, such as the Bible and the church's traditions, were being called into question. Initially, the doctrine of providence as seen through the lens of natural theology became an avenue of engagement with modern science. Christians needed a way to make belief in God reasonable in an age of rationality, and by pointing to the ordering of nature and human progress, they believed they could prove the existence of an all-powerful designer of the plan. Providence was upheld but only at the level of cosmic design, not at the level of particular events and stories about God's work in the world.

For many in Europe, the conviction that nature and history showed God's hand at work was challenged by the 1755 Lisbon earthquake and the ensuing tsunami and fires, which killed between 60,000 and 100,000 people and provoked an outcry of theological questions. Where was God? How could God let this happen? How could this be God's will? The fact that the earthquake occurred on All Saints' Day as Christians throughout Lisbon were gathering for worship provided a dreadful theological postscript to the disaster.

This erosion of belief in providence continued into the nineteenth century. In 1859 Charles Darwin published *On the Origin of Species*.[3] His hypothesis that all living creatures evolved from less complex to more complex beings devastated the proponents of natural theology because they had assumed that divine planning was the only way to account for the order found in nature. If a certain animal were perfectly adapted to live and thrive in a certain environment, natural theologians saw this as a sign that God had perfectly planned the elements of creation to fit together. With Darwin, another explanation emerged. The mutually beneficial ecosystems in which animals and plants sustain each other, while appearing on the surface to require an intelligent designer, could actually be explained by adaptation and natural selection. Those living creatures that survived over the long haul did so by adapting to their environment. Positive adaptations increased the chance of survival, while less beneficial mutations made it less likely for a creature to survive. Thus, the survivors were necessarily adapted to their environment in a way that presented a sense of order and pattern but that did not necessarily imply a Creator.

By providing an alternative account of natural order, Darwin exposed the weak foundation on which the natural theologians had built their house. One need not make Darwin an enemy, for the natural theologians had taken a big gamble on the idea that they could keep God alive as a ubiquitous and intellectually obvious public conviction. Seeking to make belief in God universally necessary, indeed universally unassailable, the natural theologians overstepped their bounds and, like Icarus with his wings of wax, veered too close to the sun. This, however, did not mean the end of providence.

The doctrine made a comeback in the period after Darwin, not as a rival theory to evolution but as an explanation of evolution itself. God was invoked as the "God of the gaps," the cosmic director of the evolutionary process, whose intervention was invoked to explain ruptures in the chain of evolution. But like previous iterations of natural theology, this attempt to make God necessary according to science would last only as long as there were evolutionary questions that science could not explain. The "God of the gaps" would inevitably be dismissed when the gaps were closed. By the middle of the twentieth century, providence—understood as God's auspicious ordering of the cosmos and God's active hand in history—was increasingly ignored in theological conversations.

### Finding the Story

How, then, might we name our conviction that our futures can be trusted to God's care, even when we cannot believe that God is the direct cause of all that happens? How can providence become a source of strength and courage in a culture of fear? To do this will mean shifting our emphasis from trying to explain suffering and evil to interpreting suffering and evil. In other words, we need to shift from a philosophical model in which we try to create the right concepts and propositions to a literary model where we try to get the story right. Providence, at its heart, has to do with the conviction that our lives and our world constitute a coherent story, a drama, in which God and humankind, together, provide what is needed to move the story toward its good conclusion. Of course, human beings often fail to participate faithfully in the drama. We act in ways that hinder the story. We often make such a mess of things that it is no longer clear there is a story at all; thus, we often experience our lives as randomness and chaos. Providence is the conviction that through it all, God's story cannot be lost.

Author Isak Dinesen once said, "All sorrows can be borne, if you put them into a story."[4] I suspect she meant that hope and healing can come from finding form in the midst of chaotic wanderings. Narrative gives form to suffering, which on its own tends toward fragmentation and isolation. Of course, in the darkness of suffering, what we need most is someone willing to recognize that the suffering has broken every structure that once gave order to our lives. Often only in retrospect can we tell the story of our suffering and situate it within a bigger story that makes our suffering something more than tragic.

Providence names the belief that ultimately we live in a story in which suffering, even death, cannot be the last word. Barbara Brown Taylor unpacks Dinesen's words this way: "There is a strange kind of comfort in a story that tells the truth about how bad things can get. . . . Plus, the very fact that someone is telling it means that you are not alone. Someone else has been there. Someone else knows what it is like, and that company—that communion—can make all the difference."[5]

Reclaiming providence as a way of telling our stories helps us address one of the dominant though subtle fears of modern and postmodern people—the fear that our lives have no purpose, which is to say that our lives have no story. We dread the possibility that we have no beginning, middle, or end, no introduction and no conclusion, no unity that would make sense of our lives. We worry that in the end our lives will seem to us and to others as just a random assortment of moments, decisions, events, and sufferings.

To borrow a cliché from the film *Forrest Gump*, we worry that "life is like a box of chocolates"—not because "you never know what you're gonna get," but because a box of chocolates is simply consumed piece by random piece until nothing is left.

Our lives, we fear, reflect the mere consuming of time, so that when we are gone we find the box has not been filled by our living but has been emptied by it.

## Figuring Out Providence

To think of providence in terms of narration rather than propositions means that we give up trying to explain exactly *how* God is present in any given event of our lives and histories. Instead, we learn to read our stories and the world's history in a figural or figurative way. By "figurative," I mean reading one thing in light of another, so that each gains new meaning by being brought together. For instance, Christians have often read certain passages from the Old Testament figuratively. The story of Abraham's near sacrifice of Isaac has been interpreted as a foreshadowing of Christ's sacrifice on the cross. Each story tells of a father handing over a son for sacrifice, and just as Isaac carried on his back the wood for the burnt offering, so Jesus carried the cross for his execution. This is one figurative way of reading the two stories in light of each other. Another way to figure the stories is to see Jesus not as Isaac but as the ram that takes Isaac's place. Here we see Jesus as the one who is sacrificed in the place of all the Isaacs, the one whose death puts an end to sacrifice.

The fact that we might figure the relationship between these two stories in more than one way alerts us to the fact that figuration is not a science but an art. Figurations of both text and history are neither hard-and-fast nor exclusive, but rather are patient of refiguring and even multiple interpretations. The process of interpreting God's activity is never finished. It is ongoing and often requires reinterpretation as events unfold. Thus, we preserve the mystery of providence while remaining confident that God will bring human history (and the whole cosmos) to its good and proper end.

The practice of reading personal history and world events in light of the stories of the Bible relies on Christians developing the skill to see things through the lens of Scripture, connecting events in the present to patterns of divine activity in the Bible. For example, in the fourth century the Christian historian Eusebius figuratively interpreted the first Christian emperor of Rome, Constantine, as a new Moses, imagining that he was going to lead God's people to a new promised land. But by the next century, Augustine painted a different picture of the Roman Empire, even in its Christian form. He interpreted its history as the unfolding violent repetition of its founding story of fratricide. As the myth goes, Romulus and Remus were sons of Mars, the god of war, raised by a she-wolf in the wilderness and destined to found Rome. But upon founding the city, Romulus killed Remus, named the city after himself, and became its first ruler. Augustine interpreted this story in a figurative relation to the biblical narrative of Cain and Abel, thus connecting the founding of Rome to the biblical story of sin, murder, and betrayal. Thus, the fall of the Roman Empire could be understood by Augustine as God's proper judgment on a people who stood for violence rather than peace.

Literary critic Erich Auerbach makes the case that reading history figuratively introduced something radically new to the way history had been interpreted before.

> If an occurrence like the sacrifice of Isaac is interpreted as prefiguring the sacrifice of Christ, so that in the former the latter is as it were announced and promised, and the latter "fulfills" . . . the former, then a connection is established between two events which are linked neither temporally nor causally—a connection which it is impossible to establish by reason in the horizontal dimension. . . . It can be established only if both occurrences are vertically linked to Divine Providence, which alone is able to devise such a plan of history and supply the key to its understanding.[6]

So the connection between two events lies not in a temporal connection (they did not happen at or near the same time, nor in a causal chain): the binding of Isaac was not a contributing cause to the death of Jesus centuries later. Rather, the connection is that both stories can be read by Christians as pointing to a vertical connection, a pattern of how God works in history.

This becomes a way of reading not just stories but current events. Auerbach goes on: "The here and now is no longer a mere link in an earthly chain of events, it is simultaneously something which has always been, and which will be fulfilled in the future."[7] Figurative interpretation rests on the belief that God is, in fact, guiding human history, and therefore the figurative connections are not arbitrary but are evidence of divine activity.

Each event, each person's story remains important, but its importance is enhanced when it becomes a sign of God's story that stretches from creation to consummation. And in God's story, the final word is life. For Jews a primary story that bears witness to this truth is the exodus.[8] For Christians the pivotal story is Jesus's death and resurrection. The stories are "paradigms" in the sense that we say of them, "Here's a story that shows how God works"—not just how God *worked* in the past, but how God *works* in the present. God does not leave Israel enslaved, God does not leave Jesus in the grave, God does not leave us in our suffering and sorrow. In God's story, no earthly event can be finally and utterly tragic. This is the deep truth of the Christian belief in providence.

We might say that learning to see divine providence in history requires learning the art of pattern recognition. Christians look for a unified plotline that holds together the fragmented events of our lives and our world. To speak of divine providence as pattern recognition does not mean that we reduce all the loose ends of historical reality to a formula. Certain things will always remain outside the story we are able to tell. To seek totality in our storytelling would be to assume that we could get a God's-eye view on things. All we can hope for is a place to stand and a way to move forward in the midst of ongoing negotiations about how to interpret the pattern rightly. Only in God's time will we see how it all holds together (or perhaps we will see that "holding together" is the wrong metaphor). Theologian Hans Frei has put the matter well:

> In this respect, as in so many others, we see in a glass darkly. But seeing darkly is not the same as discerning nothing at all. Abiding mystery is not identical with absolute unintelligibility. In our endeavor to narrate the as-yet-unfinished pattern of history, we reach for parables that might serve to set forth a kind of pattern, though not to confine history and the mysterious providence of God to these symbolic meanings. Sequences of events differ from each other sufficiently widely and always take place in a sufficiently unexpected manner so that we cannot claim that any set of images or parables can give us *the* clue to the pattern of history.[9]

We tie up what we can while acknowledging loose ends; we discern something of the pattern while recognizing that the pattern as a whole may be deeper and more complex than we ever imagined.

### Suffering, Pattern, and Providence

So how might "providence as pattern recognition" work in practice? In a powerful passage in his book *Night*, Elie Wiesel tells of the attempts made by several Jews in Auschwitz to make sense of their suffering.[10] He notes that some of his fellow inmates interpreted their suffering in terms of the biblical pattern of exile. That is, just as the Jews were punished by God with exile in the sixth century BCE, so God was punishing the Jews of Germany for their failure to follow Torah. Others rejected the idea that the Nazi horror could be God's punishment. In Wiesel's account, inmate Akiba Drumer suggested that God was testing the Jews to discover the strength and purity of their faith, just as God tested Abraham. Another prisoner, Hersch Genud, suggested that the only way to understand what was happening was to see it as the end of the world, drawing on the biblical imagery of apocalypse. Wiesel interpreted his suffering through the lens of Job. He cried out to God, lamented, and raged, just as Job did. He decried the suffering of the innocents just as Job did. He did not doubt God's existence, but he came to doubt God's justice. Yet even as Wiesel voiced his complaint, he placed himself within the Jewish biblical pattern of lament.

Each of these men struggled to see the Holocaust in a figurative relationship to some biblical story, some pattern of divine activity that would place the suffering in a narrative that would not render it hopeless. Each of these narratives gave the men hope that for them the story was not over. Each of these biblical stories ended with deliverance and redemption—God leads the Jews back from exile to rebuild the temple, God stays Abraham's hand to preserve Isaac's life, God redeems the apocalyptic end by the coming of the Messiah, and God appears to Job to restore his fortunes. The ability to narrate one's story in relation to a biblical story can provide hope that even suffering, even death, will not be the last word.

Some years ago good friends of mine were expecting their second child. But when the baby girl, Lucy, was born, physicians discovered she had a birth defect called osteogenesis imperfecta. Lucy lived only a few hours. The hopes that the parents held for this child were crushed, and we all shared in their sadness. A few weeks later we received a birth/death announcement. The small card bore the imprint of Lucy's foot. It noted her time of birth and time of death. Inside were the words, "The LORD gave, and the LORD has taken away; blessed be the name of the LORD" (Job 1:21). The words were hard to read, not just because of my tears but because I found it hard to believe that Lucy had been "taken away" by the Lord. Why would God have knit together this new life only to end it so abruptly? But I eventually realized that this was not the right question to be asking. Her parents were not making a theological claim about how God took their child. Rather, they were narrating their loss in terms of the story of Job. They were placing themselves in the shoes of Job, crying out in pain, yet holding fast to their faith and commending their daughter to God's hands. They saw in their own lives a pattern of loss and lament that had been repeated by faithful people time after time going back to Jesus on the cross, David in the Psalms, and Job in his lament for lost children.

Such figurative narration helps us to go on. It gives us words when we have no words. It reminds us that we are not alone. It situates our pain within a community. It gives us hope to affirm that this pain is not the last word. Just as Job saw God and was restored, so all of us prayed that Lucy and her parents would experience the same. Figurative interpretation of providence is nothing abstract or fancy—just the willingness to find our story in God's story and in so doing to have hope that tragedy is not the end.

## Living the Drama

Sam Wells, vicar of St. Martin-in-the-Fields in London, has suggested a particular figurative reading of the Christian story.[11] Using the analogy of a five-act play, Wells interprets the present day as the fourth act in God's drama. The first is God's creation of the world. The second is God's calling of Israel. The third is God's incarnation in Jesus Christ. The fourth is the calling

116

and sending of the church. The fifth is God's culmination of the story in the reign of God.

We live in act four. We live in a time in which God's people seek to follow God's calling in anticipation of the fifth act—the fulfillment of time and history in a new heaven and a new earth. Wells suggests that for us to continue the drama we have to know well enough what has happened in the story up until now (Scripture and tradition) that we can embody the normative patterns of the biblical stories as we move ahead. Yet we do not have the burden placed on us to make the drama turn out right. Act five lies in God's hands, not ours.

So how does this relate to providence and fear? As I noted earlier, many of us fear that our lives have no purpose beyond a set of individual choices that may not add up to much when all is said and done. But if providence names the fact that God has given the world a story and has called each of us to participate in that story, then we are freed from the fear of a meaningless life. Rather we are invited to participate in a meaning that we did not create but that, in fact, created us.

As Wells puts it, in baptism Christians "move from trying to realize all meaning in their own lives to receiving the heritage of faith and the hope of glory. They move from fearing their fate to singing of their destiny. For this is the effect of God's story: it transforms fate into destiny."[12] Once we begin to see our lives this way, we can begin to welcome the surprising and the unexpected without fear, since we know that God can weave even the darkest turns of history into the ultimate unfolding of God's good end. This is not to say that God *causes* these dark turns—God is not the author of evil. It is to say, rather, that even the darkness cannot rob our lives of purpose, since ultimately our purpose is not constructed but received. What we need, then, are communities that can help us receive and interpret these events in such a way that we transform an arbitrary fate into a promised destiny.

One of my favorite authors, Flannery O'Connor, suffered from lupus, a debilitating autoimmune disease. She died of the disease at age thirty-nine. A devout Catholic, she described her struggle this way: "My father had [lupus] some twelve or fifteen years ago, but at the time there was nothing for it but the undertaker; now it can be controlled with the ACTH. I have enough energy to write with and as that is all I have any business doing anyhow, I can with one eye squinted take it all as a blessing. What you measure out, you come to observe closer, or so I tell myself."[13] O'Connor was able to "take it all as a blessing," though only "with one eye squinted." Looked at with eyes wide open, her illness looked more like meaningless suffering or unlucky genes. Yet, as a writer, she recognized the gift that came from seeing more closely the life that was being "measured out" by her illness. In some ways our capacity to see the providing and redeeming work of providence requires this ability to look with squinted eye, to see something that is not quite visible.

Perhaps this is how my friend Bob can claim that the stroke he suffered at age twenty-six was "the best thing that ever happened to me." The stroke was part of a series of tragedies that began with his grandmother's death, continued with his mother's death from cancer, and culminated, within a year, in the stroke. These sufferings could easily have brought him to a place of hopeless grieving. They could have left him angry, bitter, and blaming God. In fact, I would not have been surprised by such a reaction. And so, the first time he told me that "the stroke was the best thing that ever happened to me," I found it hard to believe. How could such an awful, life-altering experience be thought of, even in retrospect, as good? When I asked him this question, he told me that the stroke was a crucial turning point for him, a kind of wake-up call in which he realized he had to begin to take seriously his life, his faith, and his future. The stroke set Bob on a path that he later would realize was for him a path of life.

Only the person who is suffering has the capacity and pre-rogative to find the good in their suffering. Rarely can some-one else suggest such an interpretation without appearing to trivialize the struggle. Platitudes like "It's all for the best" or "God has his reasons" may be offered sincerely, but they fail to wrestle honestly with the rupture that has occurred in the suffering person's life. What we can do in the face of tragedy is provide communities capable of sustaining those who suffer and of receiving their grief so that they might, over time, come to see their stories held within God's story.

## QUESTIONS FOR DISCUSSION

1. This chapter begins with some examples of biblical sto-ries of God's provision—the ram provided to Abraham on Mount Moriah, the manna provided to Israel in the desert, and the Holy Spirit provided to the fearful disci-ples. Are there other biblical stories of divine provision that are meaningful for you?

2. How have you understood in the past what Christians mean by "providence"? Has this belief been important for your own faith?

3. Do you find it hard to believe that God causes every-thing that happens (even evil and suffering), or does Calvin's traditional belief in providence make sense to you?

4. How can thinking about providence as a story help us get beyond the problem of either attributing evil to God (the danger of the classical view) or saying that God is not involved in this world at all (the danger of the mod-ern, secular view)?

5. What do you make of Isak Dinesen's claim that "all sorrows can be borne, if you put them into a story"?

6. Have you ever gone through a difficult time in your life in which you were able to accept with hope something that on the surface seemed only tragic? Was there a biblical story that helped you find hope?

# 8

# Security and Vulnerability

In the previous chapter we discussed the importance of thinking about providence in narrative terms. In so doing, we affirm that history is not just a series of disconnected moments and events. We affirm that each of our lives will finally be drawn into God's story so that our place in that story becomes clear. We affirm that the story is not tragic but comic, not in the *funny* sense but in the sense that all will be well, that the good hopes and intentions of the characters will not be foiled. To affirm God's providence in the face of fear is to believe that our stories, as they participate in God's story, cannot ultimately be derailed by illness or accident, evil or suffering. The fifth act has already been written and in Christ has already been enacted.

As we journey toward that good end, God promises to provide and to redeem, to give us what we need to go on and to reclaim all that is lost along the way. This is God's providential work. Providence does not mean that here and now in this vulnerable world, God will protect us from pain, harm, and danger. To think about providence as a guaranteed protection plan is to mistake both the real contingencies of life and the kind of power God uses in guiding the creation to its goal. We would be naïve to think that our faith would keep bad things from happening to us or to those we love.

## Getting beyond Faith as an Insurance Policy

There are, of course, passages in Scripture that seem to promise God's protection for the good and the faithful.

> I lift up my eyes to the hills—
>     from where will my help come?
> My help comes from the LORD,
>     who made heaven and earth.
>
> He will not let your foot be moved;
>     he who keeps you will not slumber.
> He who keeps Israel
>     will neither slumber nor sleep.
>
> The LORD is your keeper;
>     the LORD is your shade at your right hand.
> The sun shall not strike you by day,
>     nor the moon by night.
>
> The LORD will keep you from all evil;
>     he will keep your life.
> The LORD will keep
>     your going out and your coming in
>     from this time on and forevermore. (Ps. 121:1–8)

This psalm presents a biblical viewpoint that emphasizes divine protection for God's people. This voice shows up elsewhere, notably throughout Psalms and Proverbs; for instance, "Trust in the LORD, and do good; so you will live in the land, and enjoy security" (Ps. 37:3). Here the psalmist seems to promise a simple trade: if we trust God and do good, God will protect us.

Jesus speaks in similar ways when he tells the woman with the hemorrhage, "Daughter, your faith has made you well; go in peace, and be healed of your disease" (Mark 5:34). Because she has faith, she is healed. But does that mean the converse also applies—if we are not healed, it is because we did not have faith?

If we were to take these passages alone, we might come to believe that if we trust God, God will protect or heal us from all harm. While there is a strand of thought in the Bible that implies this, it is hardly the dominant strand. Indeed, on its own it can have terrible theological consequences.

Think, for instance, of the story of Job. After Job has lost his livestock, children, and health, his friends come to give comfort. After seven days of silence they begin to speak, reiterating the common wisdom found in Psalms and Proverbs—that the good will flourish and the evil will suffer. Yet Job is innocent, and he still suffers. The friends have no theological categories to make sense of this. At the end of the book, God vindicates Job and tells the friends, "My wrath is kindled against you . . . for you have not spoken of me what is right, as my servant Job has" (42:7). The book of Job complicates the issues of suffering and divine protection. Clearly, God does not always deliver the good from suffering; indeed, sometimes we suffer because of our goodness.

Dave, a friend of mine from graduate school, lost his twin brother, Steve, to cancer. While struggling against the disease, Steve received a letter from a Christian woman telling him that it was God's will for him to be miraculously healed. All he had to do was believe. Far from providing comfort, the letter struck Steve like a hot iron of judgment. If he were not healed, she implied, it would be his fault. This woman thought of providence in terms of control and protection. Because she assumed that God controlled all events, she had to justify God's apparent inaction. Her attempt to keep God blameless led her to place blame on Steve—God was ready to do the right thing if only Steve had enough faith. Though he had become very weak, Steve wanted to write a letter in response, so Dave penned the words that Steve slowly struggled to express:

> I share your faith in the almighty power of God to heal and sustain us. There may be times, though, when God's greatest miracle is not the miracle of physical healing, but the miracle of giving us strength in the face of suffering. Paul wrote in 2 Corinthians 12 that he prayed God would remove a thorn in the flesh, but God answered simply, "'My grace is sufficient for thee: for my strength is made perfect in weakness' . . . for when I am weak, then am I strong." Also, Jesus prayed in the garden that he might not suffer, but it was God's will, and he faced that suffering with a perfect faith.
>
> As I read the Bible, God's promise is to remove all our suffering in the next life, though not necessarily in this one. In this world, we will sometimes weep, suffer, and die. But in the New Jerusalem, "God shall wipe away all tears from their eyes; and there shall be no more death, neither sorrow, nor crying, neither shall there be any more pain, for the former things are passed away" (Rev. 21:4).
>
> I sincerely hope that if my cancer continues to grow, no one will see it as a failure of my faith in God, but that perhaps people can see me as faithful even if I die while I am still young. I do not claim to understand God's will, but I do know that I am in God's hands, whether in life or in death.[1]

Steve's letter revealed the fault lines in the woman's theology of suffering. She mistook God's promise to provide with a guarantee to protect, and once she had done that, she could only lay the blame for Steve's cancer at his own feet. Once she had ruled out the possibility that the cancer could result from chance or misfortune (and her understanding of providence left no room for contingency), she assumed that someone had to be blamed for the illness. Providence does not guarantee protection; rather, it assures us of God's provision (making a way for us to go on) and redemption (restoring what is lost along the way).

In the Gospels, Jesus weighs in on these issues of suffering, sin, and divine activity. He asks his disciples how they would interpret the suffering caused when Pilate killed a group of Galilean Jews while they were offering sacrifice in the temple. Did this happen because they were "worse sinners than all other Galileans" (Luke 13:2)? His answer? "No, I tell you." And recalling when eighteen people were killed in the collapse of the tower of Siloam, Jesus asks, "Do you think that they were worse offenders than all the others living in Jerusalem?" His answer, again, "No, I tell you" (vv. 4–5). And when his disciples come upon a blind man and ask, "Rabbi, who sinned, this man or his parents, that he was born blind?" Jesus answers, "Neither" (John 9:2–3). Jesus makes clear that these sufferings and tragedies did not result from sin or lack of faith. These victims did not deserve their deaths or infirmities any more than anyone else. The simplistic belief that God will always protect the faithful runs aground on the rough shore of real life. But this does not mean that God has abandoned us—which is to say that Christians could, without contradiction, place a "Shit Happens" bumper sticker next to their "God Is My Copilot" decal.

### Provision, Redemption, and Security

Divine providence does not promise "security" in the face of fear. But that is what many of us long for. We want promises that we will be safe, and if God won't give them to us, we hope our politicians will. But security often comes at a price that is too high to pay. Only by becoming invulnerable can we find absolute security, and invulnerability can be had only by building walls or destroying everyone and everything that threatens our well-being.

Our political search for security today relies on the conventional power that comes from strength and wealth. But if we believe the biblical witness, that kind of strength is no strength at all. Referring to the cross of Christ, the apostle Paul tells the Corinthians that "God chose what is weak in the world to shame the strong" (1 Cor. 1:27). He goes on to apply this to himself: "whenever I am weak, then I am strong" (2 Cor. 12:10). This paradoxical reversal of strength and weakness tells us something of God's desire to work through human vulnerability rather than to overcome it. Augustine connects this theme directly to security: "When you [God] are our strong security, that is strength indeed, but when our security is in ourselves, that is but weakness."[2] The weight of the biblical tradition lies with the view that God works through our weakness and that precisely as we seek to be "strong," we become weak. Only as we rely on God's strength in our weakness do we find real strength. The Gospel narratives display this truth in the passion of Christ. The cross reveals his power, which is the power of vulnerable love.

All well and good, you might say, but what kind of security can come from a God whose power is vulnerable love? The security that God's providence brings is the assurance of provision and the promise of redemption. God draws history to its proper end by entering the fray of human history and transforming it from within. Jesus reveals to us a God who refuses to make the world turn out right by violently enforcing the good. To do so would be to betray the good by betraying peace. God's ways are not the ways of the world. God is not a superpower or a superhero. God does not swoop in to the rescue when things get really bad.

When Pope Benedict XVI visited Poland, he journeyed to Auschwitz. "In a place like this," he said, "words fail. In the end, there can only be a dread silence—a silence which is itself a heartfelt cry to God: Why, Lord, did you remain silent? How could you tolerate all this?"³ This is the question we all want to ask in the face of suffering and evil. But even the pope confesses that "words fail" when we try to speak of such things. We have no answers that do not trivialize or domesticate the suffering. We are left with wordless lament.

What does such silence mean, in terms of our reflection on divine providence? What does it say about how God does and does not act in the world? In answer to this, we might turn to some of Sam Wells's metaphors from theatrical improvisation.⁴ In the idiom of improvisation, an actor can respond to an "offer" (an action, speech, or gesture) from another actor by "accepting," "blocking," or "overaccepting." To "accept" is to say yes and to play out the scene in the terms suggested. To "block" is to end the improvisation by refusing to continue the scene or by rejecting the premise of the offer. Blocking disrupts the scene in such a dramatic way that what follows has no coherence with what preceded. When applied as a metaphor for divine activity, "blocking" is not just God's rejection of our human "offers" but an act that violently or coercively shuts down our capacity to act meaningfully in the world. Experiences of suffering and cruelty might lead us to conclude that God refuses to "block" the world's actions, even our evil actions.⁵

In contrast, "overaccepting" indicates a willingness to receive the offer, even the evil offer, without blocking—that is, without turning to violence or returning evil for evil. But overaccepting refuses to take the offer on its own destructive terms. Rather, it takes the offer up into a larger narrative in such a way that the evil offered is overwhelmed by a bigger story and a redemptive hope. Overacceptance is another description of transforming fate into destiny.

In this sense, what my friend Bob did was to overaccept his stroke. He was powerless to block it directly, though he might have sought to block this offer by living in denial, anger, and bitterness. Instead, he overaccepted the offer: he took what happened and reframed it in a bigger story, a story in which God would not let the stroke derail Bob's aspirations. Indeed, the stroke became, in this bigger story, an opportunity to regain focus and faith in his life.

The story of Joseph in Genesis is helpful here. When Joseph's brothers attack him and sell him to slave traders, he does not block their actions, either by responding violently to them or, later, by seeking revenge upon them. Rather, he accepts his fate but transforms it through overacceptance. At the end of the story, he sees his ordeal not only as the work of his brothers but as the work of God. He says to them, "Even though you intended to do harm to me, God intended it for good" (Gen. 50:20). God acts in and through the actions of Joseph's brothers, neither blocking their evil intentions nor simply accepting them and leaving Joseph to die as a slave. God overaccepts the evil offer and thus brings about a good result (when Joseph helps save Egypt and Israel from famine) that would not have happened if God or Joseph had simply blocked the offer.

The cross of Christ is, perhaps, the most powerful example of God's overaccepting of an evil human offer. Jesus does not block Judas or Pilate or the Roman soldiers. He does not become violent, he does not draw upon his secret stock of divine superpower to save himself. He goes to his death, but he does not let death win. The resurrection is the ultimate theological overaccepting, and this tells us a great deal about how God acts in the world. If God does not use coercive power to block evil and suffering, then we should not expect God to protect us from every harm. Rather, we should seek to align ourselves with the overaccepting God, knowing that God will provide what we need to go on and will redeem what is lost along the way.

I think this is what Jesus means when he says, "Strive first for the kingdom of God and his righteousness, and all these

things will be given to you as well" (Matt. 6:33). In the context
of the Sermon on the Mount, these words appear as Jesus
is talking to his disciples about their fears and insecurities.
"Therefore I tell you, do not worry about your life, what you
will eat or what you will drink, or about your body, what you
will wear" (v. 25). Why not? Because "your heavenly Father
knows that you need all these things" (v. 32), and they will be
added. Jesus reveals that our security—that is, our provision—
emerges as a by-product of seeking God and living the way
of the kingdom. To the extent that we seek to secure our own
goods apart from participating in the kingdom, we become like
the thief who sneaks over the fence into the sheepfold rather
than going through the gate. We mistake penultimate things
(security) for ultimate things (the reign of God), and so we
seek them in the wrong way—indeed, in ways that guarantee
we will ultimately lose them. Seek *first* the kingdom of God,
we are told. Security cannot be our primary goal. Being safe
cannot take precedence over being faithful. And if being faithful makes us unsafe? If being faithful results in suffering? Then
we trust that God will provide, God will redeem our losses,
God will, in the fifth act of this great drama, reincorporate all
things in the heavenly city.[6]

### An Email Exchange

Some years ago, I received an email from a former student telling me the bad news that a friend and student of hers had
died. We exchanged several emails in the weeks and months
that followed. I include a portion of this exchange here as a
way of trying to display what it might look like to draw on a
narrative understanding of providence in the context of an
actual tragedy. This exchange gives a window into a moment
when all of this reflection on God, providence, suffering, and
fear suddenly mattered.

——Original Message——
From: Kate Brennan
Date: Friday, July 1, 2005 3:54 am
Subject: Advice

Hey Scott,

So glad I wrote you last week with a positive update of my life. Sadly, within the last week, things have taken a drastic turn, so I figured I would write and appeal to your theological sensibilities.

Since I graduated, I have been teaching private voice lessons in several local schools and have also started my own studio in which I visit students' houses weekly. I tend to get very close with my students and their families and become very much a part of their lives, as they do mine, especially the handful of young women in my own studio. My mother often calls them "the younger sisters I never had" as we are hardly a generation apart. This was very much the way my own vocal teacher worked with me over the past dozen years—often 70 percent therapist, 30 percent music instructor.

This past Sunday, I lost one of my students, Ani. She was seventeen and entering her senior year of school. We were particularly close because not only have I been her teacher, but our mothers teach at the same school and often marveled at having such similar daughters, separated by a mere five years.

It's hard to believe I felt Ani's head a bit over a week ago for a fever. By Father's Day, she was in the hospital with inexplicable symptoms—constant fever, unnatural kidney function, failing vision. . . . On Saturday, I got a call that said she had 24 hours left. I was able to visit her at the hospital several times, and hastened to make her an album of the music we worked on because the doctors said that all she responded to was music therapy. . . . When I saw her in the hospital, she was already on a ventilator and unconscious, but I spoke to her anyway.

[Since Ani's death] I've been busying myself along with my Mom in staying with Ani's Mom at her home, organizing food, answering calls, etc. I arranged the music for the services today and sang the entire mass. It was the most difficult thing I've had to do, but Ani must've helped me hold it together throughout the service. Now the funeral and burial are over; I just feel worse with each passing day.

So, naturally, I've been thinking about all of this theological stuff constantly, so I figured I'd write to you. There's no making sense of this loss. Ani emanated an incredibly positive and loving energy and was so talented, I almost feel guilty in having had her sing only for me every week.

I suppose that all those that I've lost have been my own age or older, and never my junior. I don't question or regret any time or action that I took with her; all of my students know how much I care about them and how important they are to me, and Ani must've especially known because our mothers are so close. I praised her and challenged her fittingly and I know that she was a mature, thoughtful, and convivial young woman who lived her short life to the fullest.

Nevertheless, I feel this weight—like a pile of cold wet blankets weighs on my chest and suffocates me more with every breath. I feel as if I walk in a haze and can't really comprehend how people walk around and interact and perform mundane tasks. I realize that these things take time, but I find it difficult to go into houses like hers and teach these other students, unique like her . . . but I know I have a responsibility to them (and her) to continue.

So, I guess I need some theological assurance. How do people cope with so sudden and tragic a loss? How do people find the energy to get up and walk about and drive around and make plans? How do I reassign meaning to these daily things that suddenly seem so pointless? How do I stop resenting others for having fun or placing value on things that I can see now just don't really matter? And how do I find the joy when I feel like someone has literally come in with a vacuum cleaner and sucked the joy out of my life? I've kept myself busy this week until now with plans for Ani, but where the heck can I go from here?

Anyway, I guess it's therapeutic to write. I wrote Maureen, Ani's mom, a letter about Ani and how she touched my life, which I hope provided her with what little solace one can receive at the loss of a child. And it's felt good to write to you; I'm sorry if I have bombarded you with a ton of ponderings.

Thanks in advance for listening. Hope you are well.

~Kate

—————————

To: Kate Brennan
From: Scott Bader-Saye
Date: Friday, July 1, 2005 9:32 am
Subject: Re: Advice

Hi Kate,

I'm so sorry to hear about Ani's death. It's always a crushing thing to face an unexpected death, but in one so young it's almost unbearable. I understand the experience you describe of having all the joy and meaning sucked out of everyday things. When something like this happens it seems right that the world would stop, that everyone would pause and take notice, that we would all agree that we can't return to life as usual. The very fact that the world keeps turning seems an affront to the dead and the grieving.

I have thought a lot about God and suffering, and at the very least I've concluded that the banal slogans we sometimes trot out at times like this are usually unhelpful and sometimes harmful. I've heard people, with good intentions I'm sure, say things like "God wanted another angel," or "It was her time." But we all know in our hearts it was not her time—that's the horror of it, that's why we weep uncontrollably at the loss of the young, while the death of the old allows our grief to mix with thanksgiving for a full life.

I don't believe God causes disease to take those we love. That's simply not the character of the God I've come to know through the stories of Scripture and the life of the church. God is a God of life, not death. What that means, then, is that for some reason God has chosen to allow things to happen that are not God's will. But this does not mean that God leaves us alone in our suffering and grief or that events are purely random.

As I read Scripture, and look at my own life, God's usual pattern of working is not to prevent evil and suffering but to provide a way through it and to redeem what is lost. So, although tragedy is real and painful, it is always penultimate in God's story. For Ani the last word is not death but resurrection. God redeems evil by refusing to allow it the last word, by turning even evil to good (which does not mean that Ani's death was in any way good, but that God can bring good even from evil, as Paul tells us in Rom. 8:28). It's hard sometimes to accept that good could come, because it may seem to be a betrayal of the dead, as if we could somehow conceptually make their loss "worth it." Certainly not. The good that comes is not a justification of evil or suffering, it does not make it "right" in any way; it is simply God's gift to the broken. I know, for instance, that in a particularly dark time of my life, when I felt that the suffering was unbearable, I had an experience of being "hollowed out" by the pain. This has over time created in me a space that is both emptiness and openness, so that the pain and grief of others can more easily find a place in me.

God's determination to redeem (to "buy back" or reclaim what was lost) gives us hope that in the end God's "Yes" is more powerful than the "No" of evil, suffering, and death. God provides. God redeems. But in many cases, God does not prevent. I sometimes wish it were otherwise and that God were constantly preventing evil, suffering, and death. And it is beyond me to understand how evil has gained a foothold in God's creation (though I know that in some way, small or large, each of us participates in its perpetuation). The story of cross and resurrection tells me that even the best person cannot avoid suffering, even the best life is not immune to tragedy. But, again, tragedy is not the end of the story. The ending is where God reclaims the lost, redeems the evil, restores life and goodness.

In the Episcopal burial service we say at the graveside, "In sure and certain hope of the resurrection to eternal life through our Lord Jesus Christ, we commend to Almighty God our brother/sister." I like these words because they affirm that we believe resurrection to be "sure and certain," but they are honest enough to confess that we hold this conviction as a "hope." My hope for you is that you can find hope. Not just hope in the resurrection for Ani (and ultimately for ourselves as well), but hope that over time your own ability to feel joy, see beauty, enjoy small daily gifts will return. Speaking not just as a theologian but as a person who has known pain, I believe that by some great grace, God always makes it possible for us to again say "yes" to life in a way that no longer seems a betrayal or a forgetfulness of the lost.

I wish you God's peace.

Scott

There would be no need for an email exchange such as this in a world where God protected all the good and faithful people. But that is not the world we live in. God promises to provide. God promises to redeem. God does not promise that nothing bad will ever happen to us. In fact, Jesus promises that if we follow him, the world will persecute us just as it persecuted him. If anything, we are promised suffering, but we are also promised the way through it.

Christian trust in God's providence tells us that if things haven't ended well, then they haven't ended. As Wells has noted, the simple word *and* "constitutes a significant statement. It indicates that the sentence is not yet finished. The story is not yet over. There is more to come, even when evil has done its worst. . . . If one is able to face up to a threat, stare it in the face, and say 'And . . . ?' one has gone a long way toward disarming the threat."[7]

However, the Christian affirmation of providence ought to do more than this. It cannot just be about God fixing things in the future. Providence, first and foremost, names the conditions in which we can, with courage and hope, follow Jesus now in a dangerous world. Thus, it ought to shore up our resolve to live the risks of Christian discipleship in a culture of fear. In the next chapters we will explore in more detail the practices made possible by providence.

## QUESTIONS FOR DISCUSSION

1. Have you ever wondered about the tension between biblical claims about God's provision, such as, "The LORD will keep you from all evil," and the reality of pain and suffering among good and faithful people? How have you, or those near you, learned to live within that tension?

2. Look back at the story of Steve and Dave. What do you think of the woman's view that Steve would be healed of cancer if only he had enough faith? What's wrong with this assumption? Did you find Steve's letter to be a better description of God's provision?

3. Does it make sense for Christians to believe in real contingency, real accidents in this world ("Shit happens"), while at the same time believing in God's providential care ("God is my copilot")? How might we hold these two things together?

4. Are you convinced by this chapter that God generally does not prevent evil (that is, God does not "block" our evil actions) but that God does provide and redeem

("overaccept")? How does this challenge our usual assumptions about God's power?

5. How do you think you would have answered Kate's email? Share ideas of what things we might say to those who are suffering.

## 9

# The Risk of Hospitality

I am convinced that trust in God's providence makes possible the development of the virtues—such as courage, hope, and patience—that are necessary to negotiate a broken and sometimes dangerous world in ways that are expansive, life-giving, and even a bit risky. The assurance that God's purposes for the world (and for each of us) will ultimately be fulfilled makes it possible for us to stop thinking so much about how to be safe and begin thinking more about losing our lives so that we might find them.

In one of my favorite scenes from C. S. Lewis's *The Lion, the Witch and the Wardrobe*, two young girls, Lucy and Susan, learn from the Beaver family that Aslan, the Christ-figure of the story, is actually a lion.

> "Ooh!" said Susan, "I'd thought he was a man. Is he—quite safe? I shall feel rather nervous about meeting a lion."

"That you will, dearie, and no mistake," said Mrs. Beaver, "if there's anyone who can appear before Aslan without their knees knocking, they're either braver than most or else just silly."

"Then he isn't safe?" said Lucy.

"Safe?" said Mr. Beaver. "Don't you hear what Mrs. Beaver tells you? Who said anything about safe? 'Course he isn't safe. But he's good."[1]

In making Aslan a lion, Lewis chose to emphasize the awe-inspiring grandeur of a God who cannot be domesticated. Following this God will lead us into the unknown, where safety is simply not the point. Like Abraham setting out from Ur, like the Israelites setting out from Egypt, like the disciples following a Messiah who had no place to lay his head, so Christians today follow God on a quest for fragile goodness.

The last three chapters of this book will explore ways that we might live into the risky discipleship made possible when we cease to let fear determine our lives. We will look at three of the Christian practices that are most threatened in a culture of fear: hospitality, peacemaking, and generosity.

## Beyond Suspicion

As we noted in chapter 2, the ethic of security produces a skewed moral vision. It suggests that suspicion, preemption, and accumulation are virtues insofar as they help us feel safe. But when seen from a Christian perspective, such "virtues" fail to be true virtues, since they do not orient us to the true good—love of God and neighbor. In fact, they turn us away from the true good, tempting us to love safety more than we love God.

To the extent that suspicion is seen as necessary, hospitality suffers. When the government calls on citizens to watch for suspicious activity in any public place, we become trained to see the stranger (or the strange) as threatening. In some cases, even those with different political viewpoints count as suspicious. Marc Schultz, a bookstore worker in Atlanta, tells the story of being interviewed by the FBI because of an article he was reading in a café. The agent informed Schultz that "someone in the shop that day saw you reading something, and thought it looked suspicious enough to call us about. So that's why we're here, just checking it out." And then, turning on the FBI charm, he added, "We'd just like to get to the bottom of this. Now if we can't, then you may have a problem. And you don't want that."[2] It turns out that Schultz had made the mistake of reading an article entitled "Weapons of Mass Stupidity," an essay critical of US policy in Iraq. Anxiety about terrorism led someone to believe that this behavior was troubling enough to call the FBI. We do not have to imagine political motives here to be worried by such stories.

Fear and suspicion took a darker turn in August 2019, when a young White man from the Dallas suburbs drove to El Paso with an AK-47 and began targeting Latinx shoppers in a Walmart. He killed twenty-two people. Just before the attack, the shooter published a manifesto online describing the anti-immigrant ideology that led him to violence. He wrote, "This attack is a response to the Hispanic invasion of Texas."[3] His language echoed the words of Donald Trump, who exclaimed at a rally, "You look at what is marching up, that is an invasion!" Citizens consume and digest the suspicions and hatreds of the dominant political rhetoric and then see themselves as soldiers in a war of fear. The message sent is that those who are targeted as objects of fear are to be treated as dangerous regardless of whether they pose any threat. In this case, the attitude of suspicion moved quickly to an assumption of threat and to an act of mass murder against presumed "invaders." The destructive and unfounded fear that had taken root in the shooter produced justified fear among the Latinx population in the

US. One immigrant from Ecuador said after the shooting, "It's really hard to be alive as an immigrant right now and to not be sick and exhausted. It feels like being hunted."[4]

Fear begets fear in a climate that vilifies and scapegoats difference. In such a context, hospitality to the other can get narrated by some political voices as irresponsible, dangerous, and even morally questionable. Aid groups who share water at the border or offer medical care to migrants are labeled unpatriotic and charged with criminal offenses.[5] Christian appeals to care for the stranger are easily drowned out by louder voices that profit from producing panic.

## Community as Threat to Hospitality

Unfortunately, it is not only political scapegoating that threatens hospitality. In a climate of fear, the desire for strong communities of any kind can produce a lamentable backlash against the outsider. In chapter 5, I suggested that we *need* strong communities to overcome debilitating fear. We need others with whom we can share our fears, pool our resources, and sustain our courage. But the dark side of community shows itself in the boundaries we erect to maintain our sense of safety.

The rise of populist nationalism presents a visible example of this. Anti-immigrant sentiment is not unique to the US. All over the world, nationalist movements seek to keep out immigrants and expel those who are ethnically and religiously different. This trend has been described as a backlash against the rise of cosmopolitanism in the twentieth century. The move to see oneself and one's country as a part of a worldwide community of shared and balanced interests—a vision embodied in the United Nations—has given way to a reactive focus on the purity, prosperity, and greatness of race and nation. The creation of a strong in-group sometimes comes at the cost of excluding and denigrating an out-group.

In milder and more subtle ways, this happens in church. A parish I was part of for many years liked to speak of itself as a "church family." We knew each other well, we even liked each other, and we spent time together in fellowship outside of Sunday morning. The church members cared for one another in real and tangible ways. Like any good family, we put up with the odd "relative" or two, those who carried a chip on their shoulder and now and again made trouble just to keep us on our toes. We thought of ourselves as "friendly" because we were a "family."

But in practice, friendliness and family don't always go together. It was a rude awakening to hear from members how inhospitably they were welcomed when they first arrived. Apparently, the members all enjoyed each other's company so much that newcomers were largely ignored. They were welcomed to integrate themselves into the nice family atmosphere we had created, but they needed to take the initiative to get to know us and how we do things. They should not come in with new ideas or expect us to make changes to accommodate their differences. In some ways our closeness made it all the more difficult for us to be open to others. We liked what we had, and we didn't want anyone to come in and mess it up.

Sociologist Zygmunt Bauman has written about the two-edged sword of community, especially in a fearful world where community means security. He observes, "Out there, in the street, all sorts of dangers lie in ambush; we have to be alert when we go out, watch whom we are talking to and who talks to us, be on the look-out every minute. In here, in the community, we can relax—we are safe, there are no dangers looming in dark corners. . . . We are never strangers to each other."[6] And yet, Bauman notes, this kind of community is an elusive paradise. It is what we want community to be but rarely what it is. We work hard to approximate this peaceful space, but there is a price to be paid, and that price includes the diminishing or extinguishing of hospitality.

Communities, as they really exist, often sustain their unity through their distinctiveness. According to Bauman, "distinctiveness" creates a "division into 'us' and 'them' [that] is exhaustive as much as it is disjunctive, there are no 'betwixt and between' cases left, it is crystal-clear who is 'one of us' and who is not, there is no muddle and no cause for confusion—no cognitive ambiguity, and so no behavioural ambivalence."[7] Community often demands homogeneity, sameness, and clear boundaries as a precondition for that family feeling.

In contrast to the secure sameness of the community, Bauman continues, "Strangers are unsafety incarnate and so they embody by proxy that insecurity which haunts your life. In a bizarre yet perverse way their presence is comforting, even reassuring: the diffuse and scattered fears, difficult to pinpoint and name, now have a tangible target to focus on, you know where the dangers reside and you need no longer take the blows of fate placidly. At long last, there is something you can do."[8]

Just as we long for a diagnosis when we are sick, so we long for a way to name and locate our chaotic fears. Once we have a diagnosis, we know how to respond to our illness. We feel that we can *do* something. Likewise, once we locate an object for our fear, we feel empowered. We can now take tangible steps to make ourselves safer. Insecurity is no longer the sad reality of a fallen and vulnerable world; it is the result of those people who pose a tangible and definable threat to us and our way of life. Indeed, we exist as "us" precisely because we oppose what "they" are and what "they" do. The cozy feeling of community coexists with an anxious pugnacity that arises, in many communities, as an inevitable by-product of a shared identity.

These sociological observations about human community reveal the dangers of certain church growth strategies. For instance, some manuals suggest that churches use demographic information about the areas surrounding the church to target groups who are most likely to fit in and feel welcome in their congregation.[9] Churches will grow most quickly, we are told, if they target a consistent demographic. This recipe for a homogeneous community releases churches from the hard work of offering real hospitality to the stranger, since demographic targeting makes sure that none of the newcomers are actually very different. I do not know that these church growth techniques represent conscious bias toward any particular group, but the resulting segregation by race or class suggests an unconscious desire to preserve sameness. These churches, many of which are desperate for new members to "keep the doors open," are seduced by promises of growth. Yet in a culture of fear, these strategies only reproduce a fortress mentality that allows us to feel both safe and welcoming precisely as we exclude the stranger.

Strategic analysis suggests we grow by building a community of the like-minded among those of a similar race and social status. But at the center of God's expansive kingdom is the reversal of what's seen as prudent and effective in the world's eyes. And showing hospitality to the other in a fearful world ranks high among God's nonstrategic strategies.

### Community as Context for Hospitality

So is there any way to avoid the inhospitality that forms the dark underside of many communities? Does the Christian tradition have any resources to imagine and embody communal life in ways that do not require exclusion for identity?

Christians have wrestled with these issues since our earliest days, leaving us some helpful guidance as we try to live hospitably in fearful times. First, we may be instructed by the early church council, described in Acts 15, in which the young Christian movement had to decide about the inclusion of the gentiles. Second, we may find wisdom in Paul's description of the church as the body of Christ—one body with many members, one Spirit with many gifts. Finally, we may learn to embody

143

community in the pattern of the three-in-one life of the God who is Trinity.

In the book of Acts, the early church arises from a fearful band of disciples huddled in an upper room. With the outpouring of the Holy Spirit on Pentecost, this group of followers finds courage to preach and live the way of Jesus. But it is not long before that calling produces a profound challenge to the community. Up until the middle of Acts, the followers of Jesus are clearly defined as a Jewish group marked by their belief in Jesus as the Messiah of Israel. Increasingly, however, their experience of the Holy Spirit calls into question the boundaries of the community. First, we read in chapter 8 that Philip baptizes an Ethiopian eunuch, who represents the otherness of sub-Saharan Africa and whose physical state excludes him from Jewish life, even as a convert (Deut. 23:1). Yet without regard for these two strikes against the man, Philip baptizes the Ethiopian into the community of Christ.

Next, in Acts 10 we read of Peter taking the good news of Jesus to Cornelius, a Roman centurion. Not only does Peter break Jewish law by lodging and eating with a gentile, but when Cornelius and his household believe the good news and receive the Holy Spirit, Peter baptizes them. Finally, we read later in Acts that Paul and Barnabas are received by the gentiles, who believe and follow Jesus, even as the apostles' message is rejected by their fellow Jews.

These events led the church to call its first council in Jerusalem. The point of contention is whether or not gentiles have to become Jews first in order to become Christians. This would mean laying the full obligations of Torah on the new believers, including circumcision. Neither Philip nor Peter nor Paul had demanded such full obedience to Torah for the gentiles they had baptized, and some in the Jerusalem church saw this as unilaterally altering the traditions and disobeying God. What right did these apostles have to release Christians from following

Torah? This was not just an issue of behavior; it was an issue of boundaries. Circumcision and food laws were identity markers for the Jews—they showed who was in and who was out. So the question arose: Who could be included in this new community? Could gentiles *as gentiles* be received as full members of the church?

On the one side was all the weight of Scripture and tradition. God had clearly commanded a separation of Jew and gentile in Torah. To unite the two in one community would be to ignore God's Word. Further, the Jews had for centuries maintained their identity precisely by defining themselves over against the gentile nations. How could this Jewish movement claim to be in continuity with the past if it ignored God's Word and flouted tradition? Peter, in response, tells his story about how God sent the Holy Spirit upon Cornelius and his family, claiming them as followers of Christ. Peter had very little to appeal to beyond his own experience of the Spirit, but he urged his fellow Christians to exhibit radical hospitality to those who had for so long been the excluded other.

In the end, James, the leader of the Jerusalem church, interpreted for the council the words of Amos, "I will return, and I will rebuild the dwelling of David . . . so that all other peoples may seek the Lord—even all the Gentiles over whom my name has been called" (Acts 15:16–17). Instead of reading this as a promise of the conversion of the gentiles into Jews, James read this passage as a promise to break down the Jew/gentile distinction. He then decided that the gentiles should not have to keep Torah and, most significantly at the time, gentile men should not have to be circumcised in order to join the church.

This gives Christians today a window into the radical hospitality that was necessary for the church to live into its calling in its earliest days. Welcoming the gentiles was a risky move on all counts, but the willingness of the church to take such a risk provides a paradigm of hospitality for the church today as we face our own temptations to keep ourselves safe from a hostile world.

Brian McLaren, a pastor and activist, has suggested that we shift our image of church from a "bounded set" to a "centered set."[10] "Bounded sets" are defined by a clear boundary at the edges. You are either in or out of the set. "Centered sets," in contrast, are defined by each member's relation to the center. McLaren suggests that we in the church most properly define ourselves not by the boundaries we create to define who is outside (as in a bounded set) but by our relation to Jesus as our center. The important question then becomes not "Are you in or out?" but "Are you moving toward or away from the center?"

This rethinking of what makes us "us" allows for a fuzzy border when it comes to "belonging" to the group, and it renders obsolete a simple in/out distinction. Of course, this means that we may have to live with a bit more fluidity in our identity. Without sharp boundaries we must be ready to let our identities morph over time, allowing the stranger to become friend and in so doing change in some way how we see ourselves. As Christine Pohl notes, "Boundary issues are always slightly ambiguous when we realize that God is already working in the life of every person who comes. Recognizing this opens each community to what God might be saying, what it can learn from the stranger/guest. It keeps the possibility alive that the boundaries could be redrawn."[11]

The identity issue is a hard one, because being hospitable means welcoming people into something, but if you have fuzzy boundaries, do you have a "something" to welcome people into? It seems to me that in order to avoid the dangers of being a community defined by exclusion, we have to have an identity that is always being discovered, negotiated, reinterpreted, and through Christ ever again received as gift. "Part of the difficulty in recovering hospitality," Pohl writes, "is connected with our uncertainty about community and particular identity. Hosts value their 'place' and are willing to share it; strangers desire welcome into places that contain a rich life of meaning and relationships. By welcoming strangers, however, the community's identity is always being challenged and revised, if only slightly. While this is often enriching, it can occasionally stretch a place beyond recognition."[12]

Benedictine writer Adalbert deVogüé notes that hospitality is challenging in a monastic context because of this tension between the shared identity of a close-knit community and the porous boundaries needed to welcome others. He explains these as two aspects of following Christ. "Separation and hospitality are . . . two manifestations of the same love: following Christ and receiving Christ. The following draws us out of the world, but there again he comes to us under the appearances of those who are in the world, and we receive him. Then the love which has provoked the separation is verified in hospitality."[13]

Just as the inclusion of the gentiles meant a radical rethinking of the identity of the early church, so today hospitality to the excluded other will mean opening ourselves to the possibility of learning something new about what it means to follow God in Christ.

## One Body, Many Members—One God, Three Persons

Hospitality requires that a community be capable of receiving difference as gift. One way of thinking about this kind of community comes from the apostle Paul, who often uses the metaphor of a body to describe the church. This metaphor works so well because the body has a unity that does not destroy difference. Indeed, the body functions precisely because its members are different. "If the whole body were an eye, where would the hearing be? If the whole body were hearing, where would the sense of smell be? . . . If all were a single member, where would be body be? As it is, there are many members, yet one body" (1 Cor. 12:17–20). Understanding the church as the body of Christ allows us to think of it as a place where differences can be reconciled in harmonious action. To the extent that this metaphor actually shapes our communities, Christians have an answer for Bauman's concern that no community can really exist that does not smother true difference. The question is how far we are ready to go to allow real difference in the body and to what extent this difference can be gathered into coordinated work on behalf of Christ.

The body metaphor helps us imagine a unity-in-difference that is not unlike the unity-in-difference of the God who is Trinity. Christians believe that God is one and three, one being in three persons, or one being with three "ways of being." The three "persons" of the Trinity—Father, Son, and Holy Spirit—are different yet the same. I have always been drawn to the Eastern Christian language of *perichoresis* as a description of the Trinity. While we usually translate this Greek term in technical ways like "mutual indwelling," I prefer to look back to the metaphor embedded in the concept. Since *peri* means "around" (as in "perimeter"), and *chōrēsis* means "dance" (as in "choreograph"), I like to imagine the divine life as the "dancing around" of three persons. As with any dance, the three persons must take different but complementary steps in order to keep the dance alive (in a waltz, for instance, the follow has to step back as the lead steps forward, or the dance will fall apart). The coordinated motion gains its beauty from the elegant interweaving of difference. In the very life of God is a difference that does not become competitive, an otherness that does not provoke a struggle for ascendancy. Rather, difference can be held together in a unity of purpose, in an eternal dance of love in which we are all invited to participate.

Hospitality, then, enacts not only the church's self-description of a body with many members but the church's description of God as an eternal dance of love. As we welcome the difference of the stranger, we ask how the dance might be extended to incorporate the new steps this stranger brings to us. Christians, perhaps more than others, should be ready to receive the stranger as a gift. Only as the stranger is made a friend can we know we are doing the reconciling work we have been given by Christ. The stranger is not made a friend by extinguishing the strangeness but by incorporating their difference into an ever more complex dance.

Some years ago, a young family whose primary language was Spanish began attending worship at a church pastored by a friend of mine. In response to their presence, the church decided to make their worship bulletin bilingual—printing the lessons, prayers, and some announcements in Spanish as well as English. When the family asked to have their baby baptized on Pentecost, the church celebrated with a bilingual liturgy. This small act of hospitality opened the door to visits and inquiries from other Spanish-speaking families.

When the nearby town of Hazelton passed legislation to make English its official language,[14] this church's hospitality took on political significance. The priest commented, "We have earned a reputation in the community as being a parish that has 'taken a stand' on the current immigration issues, even though our main intent was simply to be pastoral and welcoming to these new families. Of course, this hospitality has guided our parish to go ahead and make the stand, but the two are connected in ways that were surprising to us."[15] What began as an attempt to be faithful to Christ by welcoming the stranger became a witness to the alternative politics of the church.

## QUESTIONS FOR DISCUSSION

1. What do you think of the idea that God is good but not safe? Does this help you think about God in new and helpful ways, or is the idea troubling?

2. How do we find the proper balance between being safe and being hospitable? How does this relate to our discussion of courage in chapter 5?

3. Have you ever been part of a church (or visited a church) that was so tight-knit it was hard for new people to break in? Why do churches tend to become cliques? What can be done about it?

4. How does the story of the Jerusalem Council in Acts 15 help us think about issues of inclusion and exclusion today? Does it suggest any tools for how to balance the integrity of the community with an openness to the stranger?

5. Does Paul's analogy of the church as a body or the church's description of God as "three and one" help us describe the balance of unity and difference, identity and hospitality, that we are striving for?

6. Can you think of any stories of hospitality, fictional or real-life, that show what hospitality might look like today?

# The Risk of Peacemaking

One afternoon in the early days of the Iraq war, walking around the Yale campus in New Haven, our six-year-old spotted a group of people carrying signs that said, "Stop the War in Iraq" and "Bring the Soldiers Home." She was aware of the war but wanted to know more about why these people were carrying signs. We told her that some people thought we should not have attacked Iraq and that the war was unjust. There was a period of silence, and then she responded by recounting a scene from a book she had been reading. She then told us that when she got home she wanted to hand out flyers with a quote from the story.

The main characters in the story, Jack and Annie, encounter a sea serpent guarding an ancient sword. To gain access to the magical sword they must answer the serpent's question, "What is the purpose of the sword?" The children quickly try to come up with the right answer—"To defeat your enemies?" "To force them to give up?"—but neither answer unlocks the sword. Jack then remembers the instruction Merlin gave the children when they began their mission: "*Answer a question with love, not fear.*" Jack faces the serpent and his fear fades away. "'The sword should not be used to harm anyone or anything!' . . . 'The sword should not make people afraid! . . . The purpose of the sword is not fighting! The purpose of the sword is *peace!*'"[1]

With the optimism of a six-year-old, our daughter assumed that handing out flyers about overcoming fear as a path to peace just might make a difference. Small pieces of paper with "The purpose of the sword is not fighting. The purpose of the sword is peace" were handed out the following day.

It is true, of course, that almost anyone who wields the sword claims that it is in the service of peace. So the message of this middle-grade fiction may not be particularly noteworthy. But the observation that "the sword should not make people afraid" does suggest something important—that a fear-driven use of violence will most likely lead to a cycle of fear and retribution.

How can we risk being peacemakers in a fearful world? For Christians, peacemaking is not an optional side dish in God's great feast. It is at the heart of Jesus's reconciling work. Jesus blesses the peacemakers, saying that they will be called children of God; Jesus tells his followers to turn the other cheek, to love enemies, to bless those who persecute them. Jesus himself refuses to allow his disciples to defend him violently, and he forgives his executioners.

Believing that Christians are called to be peacemakers does not mean that one must be a pacifist, but it means we begin with a presumption for peace and a very limited set of circumstances in which that presumption can be overruled by a tragic and just use of force. In an ecumenical letter, the National Council of Churches called for an end to the war in Iraq. The letter included this explanation: "We certainly recognize that faithful Christians of good will may disagree with one another when it comes to questions of national policy. We trust, however, that all Christians will pray and work for peace, remembering the words, 'Blessed are the peacemakers, for they will be called children of God.'"[2] Walking in peace and practicing peacemaking are callings for all Christians, pacifists and just-war Christians alike.

## Beyond Preemption

Some of us who live in a culture of fear have become predisposed to take preemptive action for the sake of security. We have come to treat preemption as necessary and unavoidable. Since fear usually leads us to attack or contract, preemption can take either form. Some of us preemptively contract by pulling back from uncertain engagements that pose risk. In so doing we maximize security even as we diminish our exploration of life's mysteries and gifts. We praise ourselves for self-limitation, though this ends up looking a lot like cowardice. And some of us preemptively attack, seeking to destroy the source of our fear or to cause it to contract in the face of our threat. We are willing (some would say required) to strike first if it means we will become safer. If we scare others, we will not have to be afraid of them.

According to Mark's Gospel, Jesus faced the consequences of a fear-based preemptive strike. Mark tells us that the chief priests and scribes wanted to kill Jesus because "they were afraid of him" (11:18). Unreflective fear often morphs into anger, and anger sometimes rises to violence, which is meant to end the fear. But, most often, violence simply elicits fear, which produces counterviolence, which, if unchecked, spirals into a cycle of retribution. Jesus responds to those who would kill him by refusing to answer violence with violence. Jesus did not let fear of death provoke him to "preempt" the cross (not that the disciples didn't try, but Jesus told them to put away the sword—Matt. 26:52). Learning to face our fears, to share them in community, and to situate them within a story of God's

153

enduring and unfailing purposes can give us strength to break the cycle—to answer with love, not fear.

In the period building up to the invasion of Iraq in 2003, a group of Benedictine monks put out a statement about US war policy. They wrote, "As people of faith, we know that fear is a spiritual problem. Fear can only be overcome by confronting fear itself, not by eradicating every new object of fear. The answer to fear is not war, but a deep and living faith."[3] These Benedictines recognized the failure of preemption. Preemption falsely assumes that we can overcome fear by destroying every possible threat. Such a project is, in principle, interminable. In a fallen world, anyone or anything could become a threat. There is no end to preemption, which is why there should be no beginning.

## Providence as Threat to Peacemaking

I have suggested above that one of the resources Christians have for overcoming fear is our trust in the providence of God—not a naïve trust that nothing bad will ever happen to us, but a trust that in difficult times God will provide what we need and redeem what is lost. These assurances can go a long way toward relieving us of debilitating fear and helping us live joyfully. But providence has often been misused and manipulated to give divine sanction to acts of aggression and oppression.

Douglas John Hall argues that the biblical understanding of providence was distorted by a "theology of glory" intended to support and defend the triumph of Christianity socially and politically in the West. "What has happened to the biblical testimony to divine providence all too typically in Christian doctrinal history is that it has been subjected to what Luther named *theologia gloriae*—that is, religious triumphalism." Needing to justify itself, Christianity as imperial religion constructed a "triumphant providentialism" to vindicate the actions of empire. "And none of these empires learned the lessons of this providentialism more impressively," notes Hall, "than did our own North American imperium."[4] This kind of appeal to providence turns the doctrine on its head. Instead of creating a peaceful patience that trusts the future to God's hands, it produces justifications for violent domination.

Political appeals to providence often function as a divine rubber stamp for human ideologies and interests. When Rome extended its empire by conquering a neighboring state, this was taken as a sign of divine providence. When England and Spain colonized the New World, this was taken as a sign of divine providence. When the United States extended its borders to the west, this was taken as a sign of divine providence.

But if whatever happens is God's will, then whoever wins is God's winner. This distorted picture of providence would tell us that if a nation succeeds in dominating others, it is because God wants it to dominate others. Too often, the winners get to write not only the histories but also the theologies. Those who invoke providence to support self-interested aggression never seem too concerned that this puts God on the side of the strong, the rich, the privileged, and the powerful, even though Jesus's life and witness puts God on the side of the poor, the powerless, and the oppressed. We can't appeal to providence as a theological justification for imperial aggression when God in Christ resisted such powers to the point of death.

## Manifest Destiny and the War on Terror

Though many European nations have claimed divine sanction for their imperial interests, the United States emerged as the nation most committed to the mythology of a divine mandate. We even produced our own description of this mandate: "manifest destiny," a term coined by newspaper columnist John L. O'Sullivan. Urging the westward expansion of

America, O'Sullivan argued for "the right of our manifest destiny to over spread and to possess the whole of the continent which Providence has given us."[5] This justification for expansion was widely accepted, though there were dissenting voices. Note, for instance, the concern expressed in this letter to Senator Henry Clay, written by the Rev. William E. Channing in 1837: "There is no fate to justify rapacious nations, any more than to justify gamblers and robbers, in plunder. . . . We talk of accomplishing our destiny. So did the late conqueror of Europe (Napoleon); and destiny consigned him to a lonely rock in the ocean, the prey of ambition which destroyed no peace but his own."[6] Despite such minority voices, the belief that America was a "chosen nation" made manifest destiny seem almost self-evident to many Americans at the time.

At the turn of the century, American providentialism continued to guide public and political rhetoric surrounding expansion. On January 9, 1900, Senator Albert J. Beveridge argued on the Senate floor that America had a "duty" to annex the Philippines. "We will not renounce our part in the mission of our race, trustee under God, of the civilization of the world. The Pacific is our ocean."[7] And as a kind of added bonus, he noted, there just happen to be unlimited economic opportunities in China.[8] For Beveridge this was all understood as part of a divine plan for the privileging of America. "Wonderfully has God guided us Yonder at Bunker Hill and Yorktown. His providence was above us at New Orleans and on ensanguined seas His hand sustained us. . . . We can not retreat from any soil where Providence has unfurled our banner; it is ours to save that soil for liberty and civilization."[9]

Providence continues to function as a political tool, though in more subtle ways. After his administration decided to invade Iraq, Bush sought to assure the American people of a divine blessing on the war, based on a conviction that God's providence moves toward freedom: "My fellow citizens, we now move forward, with confidence and faith. Our nation is strong and steadfast. The cause we serve is right, because it is the cause of all mankind. The momentum of freedom in our world is unmistakable—and it is not carried forward by our power alone. We can trust in that greater power who guides the unfolding of the years. And in all that is to come, we can know that his purposes are just and true. May God continue to bless America."[10] In Bush's framing, America's war effort serves "the momentum of freedom" in the world that is "not carried forward by our power alone" but by the power of God, whose "purposes are just and true." This war effort, by implication, must also be just and true.

More recently, Donald Trump made a similar appeal to divine protection and American exceptionalism: "There should be no fear: we are protected, and we will always be protected. We will be protected by the great men and women of our military and law enforcement; and most importantly, we will be protected by God."[11] And if we are to believe Scott Pruitt, not only is God watching over America, God is a Trump supporter. Pruitt, who left his post as head of the Environmental Protection Agency in the midst of ethics scandals, said of Trump in his resignation letter: "I believe you are serving as president today because of God's providence."[12] Mike Pence, when asked about God's role in making Trump the Republican nominee in 2016, answered, "I believe in providence for the course of this nation."[13]

It's easy to get God's endorsement, since God rarely speaks from heaven to prove us wrong. Because of this, appeals to providence can all too easily become justifications for our own interests. And America is certainly not the first or only nation to make this claim. Political and theological voices in Great Britain, France, Germany, and South Africa have all made explicit claims to be God's chosen people.[14] Those making these claims understood themselves to be Christians, but their claims often looked more like an appeal to a partisan cosmic fate than to Jesus in all the particularity of his nonviolent witness. Once we begin to think of God in distinctly Christian ways, linking the sovereignty of God to the witness of Christ, it becomes much more difficult to justify domination in the name of providence. Since God in Jesus did not wield power to dominate, coerce, or destroy, God's providential will for the world cannot be aligned with regimes that dominate, coerce, or destroy.

In a culture of fear, we must take great care not to assume that our attempts to become invulnerable to threat are necessarily consistent with God's purposes. In fact, divine providence, rightly understood, teaches us to trust in God's future so that we may release our desire for control.

## Providence, Peace, and *Murder in the Cathedral*

The book of James links conflict and violence to our failure to trust God. James writes, "Those conflicts and disputes among you, where do they come from? Do they not come from your cravings that are at war within you? You want something and do not have it; so you commit murder. And you covet something and cannot obtain it; so you engage in disputes and conflicts" (4:1–2). What is the alternative? James goes on, "You do not have, because you do not ask. You ask and do not receive, because you ask wrongly, in order to spend what you get on your pleasures" (vv. 2–3). James suggests that our violence toward others is the result of a war within ourselves. We attack others because we sense that we do not have what we need, and this is magnified when we confuse our needs with our wants. Violence and covetousness walk hand in hand. James tells us that the solution to our violence comes from our reliance on God's care. When we believe that God will give us what we need, we can let go of our violent attempts to secure what we want.

T. S. Eliot explores the connection between providence and peace in his play *Murder in the Cathedral*, a story about the twelfth-century martyrdom of Thomas Becket, archbishop of Canterbury. As the play begins, Thomas is returning from exile in France, where he had fled to avoid King Henry II's threats. Unwilling to yield control of the church to Henry, Thomas returns to England to stand up to the throne. He has come to a point where he trusts his fate to God, knowing that even if he dies, it will serve God's cause. As the soldiers come to kill him, some of his priests bar the doors to the cathedral, but Thomas refuses to defend his life:

> Unbar the doors! throw open the doors!
> I will not have the house of prayer, the church of
>     Christ,
> The sanctuary, turned into a fortress.
> The Church shall protect her own, in her own way, not
> As oak and stone; stone and oak decay,
> Give no stay, but the Church shall endure.
> The church shall be open, even to our enemies. Open
>     the door![15]

The doors are opened and Thomas is murdered. For Thomas it is more important for the church to remain a sanctuary for all people, even enemies, than it is to save his own life.

Eliot identifies Thomas's trust in providence as the key to his courage. Just before his death, Thomas speaks to the women of Canterbury, who are already lamenting his loss:

> Peace, and be at peace with your thoughts and visions.
> These things had to come to you and you to accept
>     them.
> This is your share of the eternal burden,
> The perpetual glory. This is one moment,
> But know that another

> Shall pierce you with a sudden painful joy
> When the figure of God's purpose is made complete.[16]

Thomas knows that in some way his martyrdom will be gathered up into God's purpose, made part of God's great "figuring" of history. Only moments after this, Thomas assures his fellow priests,

> I have had a tremour of bliss, a wind of heaven, a whisper,
> And I would no longer be denied; all things
> Proceed to a joyful consummation.[17]

Here, Eliot echoes a theme from the mystical writer Julian of Norwich, a theme to which he will return several times in his later poetry, most notably in the closing movements of "Little Gidding," the last of the *Four Quartets*. There he writes (quoting Julian), "All shall be well and / All manner of thing shall be well."[18] Eliot places in the mouth of Thomas his own conviction that God's good and joyful purposes will finally be made complete. It is this conviction, this hope, that allows Thomas to let go of the fear of death.

When we trust that "the figure of God's purpose" will be made complete and that "all things proceed to a joyful consummation," we can overcome our fear of the future. We need not kill in order to feel safe. We need not make the church or the home a "fortress" against evil. Rather, we can learn to walk confidently in the steps of Thomas—not, for most of us, going to martyrdom but simply living in the peaceful way of Christ.

## Pacifism and Just War

For many, the issue of war is the most difficult problem for Christian peacemaking. Do we have a duty to support the state and its military? Is peacemaking a concern only for Christian pacifists? I would suggest that pacifism *and* just war rely on our trust in God's providence to free us from the fear that would make us use violence in unjust and unfaithful ways.

Christian pacifism rests not on a sentimental belief that if we would only lay down our arms, the other side would do the same. It does not deny that sin has distorted the world; it does not presume that the enemy will be moved by our gestures of peace. It does not suppose that we can always reach a peaceful solution through diplomatic channels. Christians do not become pacifists because they believe it will "work" better. In fact, it will likely make the world more violent, because in some instances it is only the threat of violence that holds violence in check.

The central reason for a Christian to be a pacifist—at least the central theological reason—is that one truly believes that God has made peace *with* the world in Christ and that God is making peace *in* the world through the nonviolence of Christ's followers. Only if God is actively guiding the world can Christians risk imitating the nonviolence of Jesus. Renouncing violence, then, is not a strategy for peace but a witness to the new world that is coming. Christian pacifists so trust that "all will be well" that they can risk renouncing violent means in this particular act of God's drama. In Christ, God has made a path for peace, and Christians are those who have been called to walk it without fear, precisely because we know that the fifth act has already been written.

In a similar way, Christian just-war practice rests on the conviction that God cares for the world. "Just war" names a tradition of discernment in which certain criteria have to be met in order for the waging of a war to be justified, and certain limitations are placed on how that war is waged. As Daniel Bell Jr. has pointed out, the Christian practice of just war is quite different from a governmental just-war "checklist." For

Christians, just war is a form of discipleship, a way of following God in the face of violent threat. Just war requires discipline because the extremity of the situation does not allow us simply to set aside all the virtues by which we follow Jesus—faith, hope, love, patience, courage, and wisdom. Engaging in a just war arises as a tragic exception to the presumption for peace, but it is an exception that does not render Christian identity irrelevant to the waging of war.

This takes us back to issue of fear. If we allow fear to overwhelm us, we will not be able to be faithful either as pacifists or as just-war Christians. Fearful pacifists will be tempted to fight, and fearful just warriors will be tempted to fight unjustly. Inordinate fear has a way of convincing us that effectiveness is more important than faithfulness. So if we think something will make us more secure, fear prompts us to do it, even if it runs counter to our faith. The need to put fear in its place, then, is just as important for a just-war Christian as for a pacifist. As Bell puts it, "The call to risk ourselves for others challenges us to confront the pervasive sense of fear and inordinate concern for security that threatens to envelop us. This criterion reminds us of the importance of proclaiming the gospel—that Christ has defeated sin and death, that we need not be consumed by fear, that there are worse things than dying, that we are free to live in holy insecurity, free even to die in service to our neighbor."[19]

The criteria for just war have been interpreted more or less rigorously at different times by different people. What's remained constant is that both just-war and pacifist Christians agree that there are limits to what we can do as followers of Jesus in the face of a violent threat. Both agree that Christians are not free to engage in unjust actions, even if those actions are intended for good. Christian soldiers exhibit true courage in their willingness to risk death rather than preserve their lives through unjust means. Fear, however, tempts us to ignore all restrictions on warfare in order to ensure survival at all costs:

"A people who fear death will be hard pressed to sustain just war as discipleship—for it may require facing death on behalf of our neighbor (both the victim and enemy), when fighting unjustly may offer the appearance of avoiding death. The opportunity is to recover the courage of faith, the gift of living in holy insecurity. Then we will be able to take up the cross, serving our neighbors (including our enemies) fearlessly in pursuit of a just peace."[20] It's worth remembering that fear is not always bad and fearing death is natural to all of us. Even Christians who trust in resurrection are right to fear death, since it means the loss of earthly loves. The problem comes not when we fear death (courage is only real courage if we feel fear) but when we fear it so much that we will do anything to keep ourselves safe.

Christian just war, as much as pacifism, requires a disciplined life, a readiness to risk self for others and to live with insecurity rather than to secure oneself, one's family, or one's nation unjustly. Although war may seem to be the triumph of chaos and thus without rules or parameters, the just-war tradition refuses to believe that in war everything is allowed. For Christians, even war can be waged only within the boundaries that must be drawn by faith, not fear.

## Fear, Patience, and Peace

The just-war criteria are meant to slow down the rush to war, to create dialogue and reflection. Only in this way will we avoid a fearful, knee-jerk reaction to danger. But this is no easy task, since fear teaches us to see time as a threat. Every moment seems to lead us closer to danger. "It's just a matter of time before it happens to you," is the message fear sends us—just a matter of time before you become a victim of violence, just a matter of time before you fall prey to illness, just a matter of time before you lose a loved one, just a matter of time before the markets crash. When we are afraid, time is not on our side.

Jérôme Bindé makes the case that fearfulness tempts us to live perpetually in what he calls "Emergency Time." He describes it this way: "Our era is opening the way for the tyranny of emergency. Emergency is a direct means of response which leaves no time for either analysis, forecasting, or prevention. It is an immediate protective reflex rather than a sober quest for long-term solutions."[21] Bindé helps us see how living in a state of emergency produces impatience. When large-scale destruction occurs—a pandemic, a mass shooting, a terrorist attack—we are thrown into a state of panic. But long after the event is behind us, we don't always know how to shift out of emergency time. We can get stuck in the "immediate protective reflex" that keeps us in a defensive posture. We imagine that we don't have time for "analysis, forecasting, and prevention," so we double down on more guns, more soldiers, more police; we blame others and tighten our borders, not noticing the ways that this mode of prevention can set us up for the very thing we are trying to avoid.

One of the gifts of courage is the ability to be patient because we refuse to let fear push us to act before we are ready, before we have taken time to gather the wisdom necessary to judge a situation with prudence. Christians believe that time is on our side, that history unfailingly moves toward that fifth act in which God will gather up all things in Christ. Patience, as an outworking of our trust in providence, becomes a partner of peace.

Patience is required of pacifism, since nonviolence demands the patient waiting upon God's action to bring the world to its ultimate reconciliation. Patience is also required of just war, since we cannot allow the quick obliteration of the enemy through indiscriminate killing. Yet, as Bell notes, "a culture that teaches instant gratification, that can make little sense of the patient endurance of hardship, that cannot sustain fidelity cannot sustain just war, which requires fidelity to principle and the endurance of much (even defeat!) in the name of those principles."[22]

## False Patience

At the same time, we must not confuse true patience with false patience. True patience arises from trust in God's future and a firm resolve to move toward it, while false patience arises from fear and supports the status quo. During the civil rights struggle of the 1960s, Martin Luther King Jr. wrote a letter from the Birmingham city jail addressed to eight White religious leaders in Alabama. These leaders—Catholic, Jewish, Methodist, Episcopal, Presbyterian, and Baptist—had published a joint statement calling for an end to the nonviolent demonstrations King was leading in Birmingham. They wrote, "We recognize the natural impatience of people who feel that their hopes are slow in being realized. But we are convinced that these demonstrations are unwise and untimely."[23] King's response was published in his 1964 book *Why We Can't Wait*. He wrote about his disappointment in the response of White churches and his refusal to "be patient" on their terms.

Their kind of patience was not a witness to God's providence but a weapon wielded by the powerful to shut down social change. It meant slowing down the move toward justice because some people were afraid of losing their power and privilege. It emerged from fear and fed on fear. "Be patient, or else!" was the message.

King refused to give in to false patience. He wrote, "For years now I have heard the word 'Wait!' It rings in the ear of every Negro with piercing familiarity. This 'Wait' has almost always meant 'Never.' We must come to see, with one of our distinguished jurists, that 'justice too long delayed is justice denied.' . . . There comes a time when the cup of endurance runs over, and men are no longer willing to be plunged into the abyss of despair. I hope, sirs, you can understand our legitimate and unavoidable impatience."[24]

Despite King's clear and persuasive challenge to White versions of "patience," he embodied and encouraged another kind of patience. Rooted in his commitment to nonviolence, King refused to engage in an impatient call to arms. In his "I Have a Dream" speech, delivered on the steps of the Lincoln Memorial during the summer of 1963, King spoke of "the fierce urgency of now" and decried "the tranquilizing drug of gradualism." Yet he followed these words with a caveat: "But there is something that I must say to my people who stand on the warm threshold which leads into the palace of justice. In the process of gaining our rightful place we must not be guilty of wrongful deeds. Let us not seek to satisfy our thirst for freedom by drinking from the cup of bitterness and hatred. We must forever conduct our struggle on the high plane of dignity and discipline. We must not allow our creative protest to degenerate into physical violence."[25] King refused the kind of impatience that would trade righteous urgency for the violence justified by emergency. His commitment to nonviolence meant that he was willing to take the time necessary to pressure and persuade the White population to change. He recognized that White freedom and Black freedom were "inextricably bound" and that "we cannot walk alone."[26] Real transformation would require the kind of patience intrinsic to nonviolent action, the patience that seeks to change the heart of the oppressor and not just the law.

King's active patience was rooted in his belief in providence, his trust that "there is a creative force in this universe, working to pull down the gigantic mountains of evil, a power that is able to make a way out of no way and transform dark yesterdays into bright tomorrows." And so, he added, "Let us realize that the arc of the moral universe is long, but it bends toward justice."[27] Such conviction gave King the courage and the hope necessary to work for reconciliation and not merely victory.

In a fearful culture, we will be tempted to act precipitously, which often means acting to control, coerce, or dominate. But that fearful push toward the rushed solution robs us of the patience we need to seek the right solution. As we learn to loosen the grip fear has on us, we will find ourselves able to embrace the patience necessary to be peacemakers. We will not be taken in by the rhetoric of "emergency time" that demands the quick (and often violent) fix. Nor will we be taken in by the rhetoric of false patience that urges inaction out of a fearful resistance to change. Only as we begin, once again, to trust the future will we be able to renounce unjust violence and false patience in order to embrace the vulnerable and patient discipline of peacemaking.

## QUESTIONS FOR DISCUSSION

1. How does fear make it difficult to live peacefully? Why do you think preemption is such a strong temptation?

2. Do you think most Americans believe that God is providentially guiding our country? Is there a way of holding that belief without using it as a political tool?

3. In T. S. Eliot's play *Murder in the Cathedral*, Thomas Becket tells the women of Canterbury that they have to bear their "share of the eternal burden," which is also "the perpetual glory." But, he says, this burden/ glory is just "one moment," and another moment "shall pierce you with a sudden painful joy / When the figure of God's purpose is made complete." How do you interpret these lines? What is the burden we have to bear? What is the "figure of God's purpose"?

4. Take a look at some of the Scriptures mentioned in this chapter: James 4:1–3 and Matthew 26:47–52 (see

the parallel account in Luke 22:47–51). How do these passages speak to the issues of fear, violence, and peacemaking?

5. Why is patience so important for peacefulness? What makes it difficult for you to be patient? What could the church do to help its members develop patience?

6. How can we tell the difference between the true virtue of patience, which helps us be peaceful, and false patience, which refuses to work for change?

# 11

# The Risk of Generosity

One afternoon, after sharing a meal with some Pharisees, Jesus strolls outside to find a crowd of thousands gathered to see him and to hear his teachings. Someone in the crowd shouts out a request, "Teacher, tell my brother to divide the family inheritance with me" (Luke 12:13). But Jesus refuses to become the arbiter. Instead, he tells the man, "Take care! Be on your guard against all kinds of greed; for one's life does not consist in the abundance of possessions" (v. 15). He then tells the crowd a parable about a rich man whose land produced well beyond his expectations. The man was thrilled but faced a problem. He did not have enough space to store all the excess crops. So he decided to raze his current barns and build new, bigger ones in their place. Once all of his goods were safely stored away, he would take his rest and say to himself, "Soul, you have ample goods laid up for many years; relax, eat, drink, be merry!" (v. 19). But that very night he died.

The parable does not suggest that God killed the man for being greedy. Rather, the man's hoarding, meant to secure his

future, ended up securing nothing. Jesus teaches that possessions are not what makes life worth living and that they cannot
preserve or extend life. The upshot of the parable seems to be,
"You may be rich, but you're still dead."

Jesus's attitude toward the rich fool, however, is not one of
disdain but compassion. This is not a parable of judgment. It
is a parable about someone who wrongly believed that great
possessions could secure his future. It is a parable about fear
and security and where true security lies. This message becomes
clear if we read on in Luke's Gospel, for immediately following
this parable Jesus says, "Therefore . . . do not worry about your
life, what you will eat, or about your body, what you will wear.
For life is more than food, and the body more than clothing. . . .
And can any of you by worrying add a single hour to your
span of life? If then you are not able to do so small a thing as
that, why do you worry about the rest? . . . Do not be afraid,
little flock, for it is your Father's good pleasure to give you the
kingdom" (12:22–32).

Jesus seeks to dispel the illusion that wealth can prevent
misfortune. When we trust in God's provision, we are able to
release our fear of not getting by and so release our grip on
possessions. "Strive for [God's] kingdom," Jesus tells the crowd,
meaning, among other things, "Sell your possessions, and give
alms." And if you do this, then "these things"—food, clothing,
security—"will be given to you as well" (12:31–33).

## Beyond Accumulation

As we have seen, the ethic of safety fosters the false virtues of
preemption and suspicion. There is one more false virtue that
we must unmask—the unbridled accumulation of wealth. In
fearful times we understandably wish to gather up whatever
resources we can find. Biblical scholar Walter Brueggemann
notes that "the fundamental human condition continues to be

anxiety, fueled by a market ideology that keeps pounding on us to take more, to not think about our neighbor, to be fearful, shortsighted, grudging. . . . Whether it's global policies or local poverty-wage jobs, those who fear scarcity refuse to acknowledge any abundance that extends beyond their own coffers."[1]

Like the rich man in the parable, we imagine that accumulating wealth will make us more secure. And there is some truth in this. When we have inadequate resources, we rightly fear that the future may bring misfortunes that we can't handle or bills that we can't pay. And these are legitimate concerns. In most cases, saving—for an emergency, or college, or retirement— reflects prudence and good stewardship of resources. The capacity to save reflects an ability to delay gratification and to resist the lure to buy more and more. So the problem is not savings as such.

The problem arises when our fear becomes excessive so that we can no longer make good judgments about what is enough, or when it causes us, in Aquinas's terms, to "renounce that which is good."[2] When we are so intent to avoid harm to ourselves that we neglect to do good to others, then we have lost the battle with fear.

## How Providence Threatens Generosity

If we Christians are to learn to hold our wealth loosely and share our goods generously, we have to overcome inordinate fear. Trust in providence is one way Christians stave off fear. However, just as providence has been misused as a theological defense of violence and imperialism, so providence has been misused to justify the unbridled pursuit of wealth. Unless we can combat this divine cover for greed, we will never develop the freedom to give generously as a Christian response to God's provision.

Adam Smith, an eighteenth-century Scottish moral philosopher, believed that there were laws of economic life, just as there were laws of nature. And these economic laws worked in such a way that by seeking one's own wealth, one made others wealthier and more secure. Or to put it theologically, God so orders the means of economic provision that the pursuit of one's own good in turn does good to others. In *The Wealth of Nations*, Smith describes this idea in relation to the modern capitalist:

> By preferring the support of domestic to that of foreign industry, he intends only his own security; and by directing that industry in such a manner as its produce may be of the greatest value, he intends only his own gain, and he is in this, as in many other cases, led by an invisible hand to promote an end which was no part of his intention. Nor is it always the worse for the society that it was not part of it. By pursuing his own interest he frequently promotes that of the society more effectually than when he really intends to promote it.[3]

Smith created the perfect economic philosophy for the modern age—unlimited and guilt-free accumulation. This economic principle was based on Smith's assumption that when we promote our own gain or security, we benefit others as a by-product. So, for instance, the desire for wealth drives people "to cultivate the ground, to build houses, to found cities and commonwealths, and to invent and improve all the sciences and arts, which ennoble and embellish human life."[4] The goods of society and culture, including things like medicines, roads, and schools, come into being because of the efforts of self-interested individuals, who in turn serve others.

Smith went on to theorize that since a person can only consume so much of the earth's produce—noting that one person's stomach cannot hold substantially more than another person's—even the rich landowner who harvests thousands of acres for his own gain can partake of only a small portion of that production. "The rest he is obliged to distribute among those, who prepare, in the nicest manner, that little which he himself makes use of, among those who fit up the palace in which this little is to be consumed, . . . all of whom thus derive from his luxury and caprice, that share of the necessaries of life, which they would in vain have expected from his humanity or his justice."[5] In other words, the livelihoods of all those who serve the rich man are dependent upon his continuing to seek greater and greater wealth, which, because he cannot consume all he produces, will inevitably trickle down for their benefit. And these scraps from the table are likely more than this man would have given if one simply appealed to his "humanity or his justice."

Smith describes this process as the working of an invisible hand, a kind of providence, that keeps the economic balance even as we all live self-interested lives. He writes that the wealthy "are led by an invisible hand to make nearly the same distribution of the necessaries of life, which would have been made, had the earth been divided into equal portions among all its inhabitants, and thus without intending it, without knowing it, advance the interest of the society."[6] Again, Smith exhibits a remarkable trust in the combined effects of the market and the natural limits of human consumption to create an equal distribution of goods among people. "When Providence divided the earth among a few lordly masters, it neither forgot nor abandoned those who seemed to have been left out in the partition. These last too enjoy their share of all that it produces."[7]

Contrary to classical or Christian moral theory, Smith suggests that one can serve the common good without the virtues of charity, temperance, self-control, or justice. Indeed, he suggests we might even serve the interests of society best when we are not explicitly trying to do so. Smith's theories have produced what theologian John Milbank has called the "de-ethicization" of the economic.[8] Rather than reflecting on the moral issues involved in making and spending, producing and consuming, Smith's theories appealed to providence to explain "how bad or self-interested actions can have good long-term outcomes."[9] Thus, we need not entertain ethical questions, since equity and justice should naturally work themselves out.

Rather than strengthening a courageous and patient life of Christian discipleship, Smith's providence made traditional morality seem archaic and unnecessary. Interpreted through this lens, providence assures us that God will take care of the poor if we just take care of ourselves. One of the ironies here is that by bringing God *into* the discussion of economy, by appealing to the doctrine of providence, Smith made it more difficult to use providence to critique the market. The language had already been captured.

We might note briefly that capitalism, understood as an unrestrained free market, does not seem to function the way Smith thought it would. Perhaps the invisible hand has gotten tired of working its magic. As far back as the time of Jesus, people were aware that the goods of the wealthy did not necessarily trickle down to others just because the rich had produced more than they could consume. Rather, humans are inclined to build bigger barns, to find ways to store and amass goods for the future, since one might need little but want much. Especially when fear of the future combines with self-interest, we cannot expect that the pursuit of gain will result in an equitable distribution of goods, even for basic needs.

## Provision, Abundance, and Generosity

Before the rise of modernity and capitalism, the doctrine of providence did not constitute a social safety net that freed us from moral obligations to one another. Rather, providence was meant to assure us of God's continuing care for us so that we might share generously with others.

Genesis offers an interesting example of the tension between trusting God's care and exploiting others for personal gain.[10] Genesis begins with abundance and ends with scarcity. It begins with God's abundant creation. It ends with a famine that drives the Israelites to Egypt to avoid starvation. The movement from abundance to scarcity creates the opportunity for God's people to decide how they are going to handle the threat of "not enough." The text recognizes that the real issue is not scarcity produced by famine, but what humans are willing to do in the face of that scarcity.

In the narrative, Joseph, one of Jacob's twelve sons, has been sold by his brothers into slavery. The slave traders take Joseph to Egypt, where he is arrested and jailed on false charges. Ultimately, Joseph gains his freedom because God has gifted him with the ability to interpret dreams. As it turns out, the Pharaoh needs just such a person. Joseph's interpretation of Pharaoh's dreams suggests that there will be a period of abundance followed by a period of famine. In response, Pharaoh asks Joseph to create a plan to keep the people fed during the lean years. So far, so good. God has made it possible for Joseph and Pharaoh to prepare for the coming scarcity in such a way that God's abundant provision will be enough.

The story takes a dark turn as Joseph and Pharaoh choose to exploit scarcity to gain more for themselves. Their scheme works like this: For seven years Joseph collects one-fifth of the produce of the land and stores it away in advance of the coming lean years. When the famine hits, Joseph sells a portion of the extra grain back to the people of Egypt and Canaan for exorbitant prices. Genesis says he "collected all the money to be found in the land of Egypt and in the land of Canaan, in exchange for the grain" (Gen. 47:14). The next year, Joseph requires payment of "all their livestock" in exchange for the grain (v. 17). The following year, as the famine continues, Joseph requires the people to give up all their land and finally to sell themselves into slavery to Pharaoh (vv. 20–21).

What begins as a plan to share the abundance of God ends as a plan to exploit scarcity so that Pharaoh can accumulate all the wealth, land, and bodies in the kingdom. Joseph, as Pharaoh's partner, effectively collects the excess from the people for seven years only to sell their own extra produce back to them at such an exorbitant rate that they are forced to become slaves in order to eat. The truth is, there was no real scarcity. God's provision created enough abundance to carry the people through the drought.

Walter Brueggemann interprets Pharaoh's actions this way: "Because Pharaoh . . . is afraid that there aren't enough good things to go around, he must try to have them all. Because he is fearful, he is ruthless."[11] The contrast between God's abundance and our fear of scarcity is a defining issue for us today. If we are incapable of trusting God's abundance, then we will take advantage of the threat of scarcity to line our own pockets. In contrast, if we believe that God can and will provide abundantly, then we will be able to "live according to an ethic whereby we are not driven, controlled, anxious, frantic or greedy, precisely because we are sufficiently at home and at peace to care about others as we have been cared for."[12] Trusting providence means trusting God's provision, and trusting in God's provision allows us to embody generosity.

After Moses brings the enslaved Israelites to freedom across the Red Sea, the Bible tells a different story of scarcity and abundance. As the Israelites are wandering through the desert, making their way to the promised land, they grow tired and hungry. Some of them even want to turn back to Egypt. The hot, dry desert is a place of scarcity, and even though Egypt was a place of oppression, at least they had food. So God tells Moses, "I am going to rain bread from heaven for you, and each day the people shall go out and gather enough for that day"

(Exod. 16:4). God answers scarcity with abundance but makes very clear that the abundance depends on the Israelites' practicing restraint. Each person is to gather only as much bread, or "manna," as he or she needs and to leave the rest for others. In this way, God promises there will be enough.

Many of the Israelites did what God commanded, "some gathering more, some less. But when they measured it . . . those who gathered much had nothing over, and those who gathered little had no shortage; they gathered as much as each of them needed" (Exod. 16:17–18). Yet some of the Israelites tried to gather more than they needed, to save and accumulate for later. Not only did this leave others hungry; it proved wasteful, since the extra bread spoiled overnight—it "bred worms and became foul" (v. 20). In God's economy, hoarding would not be rewarded.

This story is a parable of trusting divine provision. God's economy is sufficient, even in the midst of apparent scarcity. It teaches us that we subvert abundance when we gather more than we need while others have less than they need. "Trust in God's providence therefore involves not only an expectation of sustenance," writes Christopher Franks, "but also a yielding of ourselves, whereby we conform our demands for sustenance to the temporally unfolding determination of that provision."[13] In other words, providence is not only about God providing for our needs but also about our learning to need no more than God provides.

Paul uses similar logic to encourage the Corinthians to contribute to the offering for the poor in Jerusalem. He assures them, "God is able to provide you with every blessing in abundance, so that by always having enough of everything, you may share abundantly in every good work" (2 Cor. 9:8). God gives abundantly so that they will know the joy of sharing God's gifts with others. As in the story of manna in the desert, the reality of abundance for all requires that we participate in justly distributing everything that God provides.

John Calvin has been charged with paving the way for modern economic shifts, opening theological space for a free market and lending at interest. Whether or not this is a fair assessment, Calvin undoubtedly connected God's generosity with radical economic sharing. This path of generosity begins, he affirms, when we acknowledge that "all the gifts we possess have been bestowed by God and entrusted to us on condition that they be distributed for our neighbors' benefit."[14] Here Calvin echoes Aquinas, who made the similar point that human beings "ought to possess external things, not as [their] own, but as common, so that, to wit, [they are] ready to communicate them to others in their need."[15] Our goods come to us conditionally; thus, nothing we have may be considered our own in any ultimate sense. Scripture and tradition support the idea of *personal* property but not *private* property; that is, property may be personal in the sense of being under my control, but it is not private in the sense that what I do with it is purely my concern. If "the earth is the Lord's and all that is in it" (Ps. 24:1), then all human ownership is really stewardship—a trust to manage the goods of another.

Calvin notes, "Scripture calls us to resign ourselves and all our possessions to the Lord's will." Of course, part of "the Lord's will" involves meeting the needs of our household. So how much do we need? According to Calvin, we must first "yield to [God] the desires of our hearts to be tamed"[16] if we are going to be able to distribute our gifts for our neighbors' benefit. For until we learn to temper our desires, to know the difference between wants and needs, we will always find justification for gratifying our wants while others go without needs.

## Control or Flow?

So if we were to reclaim the practice of generosity in this culture of fear, what would that generosity look like? Is generosity the same as giving charity, or, as they used to say, "almsgiving"? Certainly generosity needs to include a voluntary redistribution of resources from those who have more than they need to those who have less than they need. But charity can have unintended consequences. First, we may use charitable giving as an excuse not to change social arrangements that make it difficult for the poor to break out of poverty and attain the dignity of self-supporting work (as when a large corporation makes substantial donations to local charities rather than paying a living wage). Second, charitable giving may produce a patronizing relationship in which the giver remains disconnected from the need and the receiver is deprived of agency.

The biblical story of two brothers, Cain and Abel, provides some interesting reflections on care and responsibility. After murdering Abel, Cain asks God, "Am I my brother's keeper?" (Gen. 4:9).[17] Some of us still assume that the answer is yes, although increasingly this is a minority view. We sometimes hear people quote this passage as a way of calling us to a proper concern for the welfare of our fellow human beings. But the biblical text suggests something different is going on. The word "keeper" is never used in Genesis (or anywhere in Torah) to describe something humans should do or be for each other. Human beings "keep" flocks or "keep" the covenant, but they do not "keep" each other. By contrast, God alone is described as "keeping" people, such as when God tells Jacob, "Know that I am with you and will keep you wherever you go" (28:15). So Cain seems to be reminding God that God is his brother's keeper and that God, not Cain, should be watching out for Abel. If something has happened to Abel, Cain implies, it's God's fault. Cain thus speaks a half-truth. By throwing back on God the responsibility of "keeping" Abel, Cain rightly recognizes that we cannot be God to each other, but falsely assumes that this fact releases him from responsibility.

When we think of practicing generosity or charity, we have to be careful not to imagine ourselves as our brother's keeper, thus asserting a control over the other that is not rightly ours. But neither should we imagine that since God is our brother's keeper, we have no moral obligations. The abundance of provision comes from God alone, but God relies on us to participate in God's abundance in such a way that we do not hoard the blessing. We have a part in keeping the blessing flowing, in becoming a conduit for God's abundance. Which is to say we are called to be our brother's brother, our sister's sister, so that God can be their keeper.

Rightly understood, divine providence frees us of our illusions of control for the sake of God's abundant charity. Generosity is how we participate in the "flow" of that provision. It happens when we release control and get caught up in something bigger than ourselves. It happens when we come to see ourselves as a portal of divine abundance. It happens when we invite others to participate in the unhindered flow of God's goods.

## Generous Business

This vision of generosity is not simply personal or private. Today we need examples of people carrying this trust in abundance, this flow of generosity, into their business practices. Again, I don't simply mean that businesses should make large donations to worthy causes (though that's not a bad thing); rather, I mean businesses should build the habits of generosity into the process of producing and selling goods. We need to be able to see, describe, and imagine doing business in such a way that we refuse to make profit our highest goal, thus focusing our work on the shared good that is created for both the producers and the consumers. Generous business—or "humane capitalism" or the "economy of communion"[18]—refuses to create wealth for some at the expense of others but instead trusts that there is enough for everyone.

As consumers we can provide intentional support to businesses that occupy a space between traditional for-profit and nonprofit institutions.[19] These include benefit corporations, credit unions, cooperatives, and community-supported agriculture. Social enterprises can contribute significantly to the reduction of economic inequality. In an interview, Josu Ugarte, the president of the world's largest cooperative, the Mondragon Cooperative in Spain, noted, "Our solidarity in terms of salaries changes the distribution of wealth in society. If the Basque region in Spain were a country, it would have the second-lowest income inequality in the world."[20] Such a large-scale enterprise is both remarkable and heartening. There are also small-scale models of social entrepreneurship that imagine business and profit in a different way.

In 1995 in the San Francisco Bay area, a new online classified service was launched. It began as Craig Newmark's list of activities going on in the Bay Area. Over time the list grew, and when Newmark wrote software that could turn emails into web posts, he opened the site to postings from others. The site, craigslist.org, quickly became a nexus for thousands of job listings, apartment rentals, items for sale, personals—typical classified material. In addition, the site created community through discussion forums and occasional face-to-face parties.

What made this site different from other such services was that Newmark didn't charge anything, nor did he allow ads on the site. At that point, the endeavor made no money. In 1997 he was approached by Microsoft Sidewalk with an offer to run banner ads. Though he could have quit his day job and lived off of the revenue of that one customer, Newmark declined the offer.[21]

In 1999 he decided to devote all his energy to Craigslist and turned it into a for-profit company. Holding on to the goal of providing a noncommercial environment, Newmark still did not allow advertising. Instead, he began to charge minimal rates (well below market value) for job listings in San Francisco, Los Angeles, and New York. Because of the incredible volume of the site, that income alone supported the company. Over time Craigslist has begun charging for job listings in all US cities and charges for a few other for-profit categories such as New York City apartments and automobile ads placed by dealers. Most other categories remain free. Newmark has long refused to maximize profit, though he makes plenty. Back in 2004 a *New York Times* headline summed up Newmark's business model: "Craig's To-Do List: Leave Millions on the Table."[22] Today, analysts suggest that Craigslist could increase revenue tenfold without anyone complaining, but Newmark's business model has remained simple: charge those with substantial resources, make it free to everyone else, and refuse all advertising.[23]

Why does he leave money on the table? As Newmark has put it, "some things should be about money, some shouldn't."[24] He has credited his "Sunday school and Hebrew teachers, Mr. and Mrs. Levine," for teaching him how much is enough.[25] He has been known to say that the one thing he lacked was a regular parking place, but after moving to a new house, he observed, "the only thing I've been lacking is a hummingbird feeder that actually works."[26]

Craigslist is not perfect, and it has been rightly challenged to take responsibility for ads that connect people who have malicious or criminal intent. Further, Newmark has been blamed, fairly or not, for contributing to the downfall of newspapers by helping dry up revenue from print classifieds. Nonetheless, Craigslist exemplifies a way of doing business that refuses to maximize profit at all costs. He has remained true to his mission to provide a free—and ad-free—service to millions of people while only charging the wealthiest users. He trusted that there would be enough and that doing business could be a way of building community.

## Sabbath Living

Surely Mr. and Mrs. Levine did not have any idea that they were helping shape how a billionaire would one day think about his money. But that very fact serves as an inspiration for churches (and synagogues) to continue to be intentional about teaching temperance and generosity. Traditionally, Sabbath keeping was one way of doing this. The challenge, though, is to extend Sabbath from a single day into a way of living, a daily trust in God's abundance. Brueggemann writes,

> As shown in the creation account, Sabbath (God's day of rest) is based on abundance. But how willing are we to practice Sabbath? A Sabbath spent catching up on chores we were too busy to do during the week is hardly a testimony to abundance. A Sabbath spent encouraging those who want to fill our "free time" with calls to amass more possessions—whether the malls with their weekend specials or televised sports events with their clutter of commercials—does nothing to weaken the domain of scarcity. Honoring the Sabbath is a form of witness. It tells the world that "there is enough."[27]

Sabbath keeping is a way of practicing providence, of enacting the belief that God will provide. One day each week, we give up providing for ourselves. On this day, we practice the kind of reliance on God that can sustain our generosity throughout the rest of the week. At its best, a Sabbath day gestures beyond itself to other habits and practices that support God's economy in everyday living.

For the ancient Israelites, one of these practices was the sabbatical year (Exod. 23:10–13; Lev. 25:1–7; Deut. 15:1–18). Every seventh year, the Israelites were commanded to let their fields lie fallow. In this year, the poor and the wild animals were given free access to whatever the land produced. Further, within the community of God's people, all debts were wiped clean and all slaves were set free. In addition to the Sabbath day and the sabbatical year, there was one more grand gesture of God's abundance built into Israel's Torah—the Jubilee Year. This was a Sabbath of Sabbath years—seven times seven years. In this forty-ninth year, not only did all the sabbatical-year regulations apply, but all land was returned to its original owner. If a family had fallen on hard times and had to sell their land to buy food or pay debt, the Jubilee Year ensured that this would not create for that family a cycle of poverty extending through many generations. Rather, every Jubilee provided a chance to start over; every Jubilee broke the back of poverty and returned to all the people the means of production. The central features of the Sabbath economy, rest and plenty, were evident throughout Israel's economic life.

The goal of these practices was a periodic restructuring of the economy so that the gap between rich and poor would not continue to grow unchecked. In the context of explaining the sabbatical regulations, Moses tells the people, "There will, however, be no one in need among you, because the LORD is sure to bless you in the land that the LORD your God is giving you as a possession to occupy, if only you will obey the LORD your God by diligently observing this entire commandment that I command you today" (Deut. 15:4–5). Note the "if only"—God's promise of provision is based on Israel's willingness to live in a Sabbath-based economy—that is, an economy of abundance and trust. The text goes on to say that when an Israelite releases a slave in the sabbatical year, they are to be provided for: "You shall not send him out empty-handed. Provide liberally out of your flock, your threshing-floor, and your wine press, thus giving to him some of the bounty with which the Lord your God has blessed you" (Deut. 15:13–14). The abundance of God is to be held lightly, permitted to flow through the hands of those who have much to bring blessing to those who have little.

The Eucharist recalls and enacts the logic of divine abundance that permeates the sabbatical regulations. Echoing the feeding of the multitudes, Jesus at the Last Supper took bread, gave thanks, blessed the bread, and broke it. And as he broke the bread and gave it to others, there was enough—enough for the five thousand hungry followers, enough for the twelve disciples, enough for us. The bread and wine of Communion is a continuation of Jesus's miraculous provision whereby he, himself, becomes our food. It is a foretaste of God's heavenly feast and a promise that God's provision will never be lacking. But, as we have seen, this divine provision is enough for all only if we do not subvert God's abundance by hoarding the blessing. Christians are sent from the Eucharist to share with the world what we have received at the table—bread broken and enough for all. We are sent to tell the world, "Do not be afraid . . . for it is your Father's good pleasure to give you the kingdom" (Luke 12:32).

## QUESTIONS FOR DISCUSSION

1. Read through some of the biblical passages cited in this chapter (Gen. 47:13–26; Exod. 16:1–30; Lev. 25:1–7; Deut. 15:1–18; Luke 12:13–34). How does Scripture invite us to think about wealth, work, economy, and generosity, especially in relation to our fears about having (or not having) enough?

2. How do you determine what is enough when it comes to the accumulation of wealth through savings and investments? Do you have anyone you can talk freely with about stewardship of money? Why do you think

Americans are so reticent to talk about personal fi-
nances (how much we make, spend, save, and give)?

3. In a culture of fear, we are all the more tempted to be
controlling—to control our money, to control other
people, to control the future. How does providence help
us release control? What church rituals or sacraments
help us practice giving up control? How does giving up
control help us become generous?

4. Can you think of examples of everyday generosity from
your life or others you know? How might we let God's
abundance flow through us in ordinary living?

5. This book begins and ends with the biblical words,
"Do not be afraid." Having read this book, how do you
imagine you might become less fearful? How can Christians live in the world in such a way that we help others
around us to be less fearful?

# NOTES

## Preface

1. Pope Francis, "Address of His Holiness Pope Francis to Participants in the 3rd World Meeting of Popular Movements," November 5, 2016, Vatican website, http://w2.vatican.va/content/francesco/en/speeches/2016/november/documents/papa-francesco_20161105_movimenti-popolari.html.

2. Donald Trump, quoted in Bob Woodward, *Fear: Trump in the White House* (New York: Simon and Schuster, 2018), xiii.

3. Marilynne Robinson, *The Givenness of Things* (New York: Farrar, Straus and Giroux, 2015), 126.

## Chapter 1: Fear for Profit

1. Frank Furedi, *Paranoid Parenting* (Chicago: Chicago Review Press, 2002), 12.

2. Centers for Disease Control and Prevention, "Sudden Unexpected Infant Death and Sudden Infant Death Syndrome: Data and Statistics," CDC, accessed October 10, 2019, https://www.cdc.gov/sids/data.htm.

3. *Finding Nemo*, DVD, directed by Andrew Stanton and Lee Unkrich (Buena Vista Pictures, 2003).

4. Lenore Skenazy, "Why I Let My 9-Year-Old Ride the Subway Alone," *New York Post*, April 1, 2008, https://www.nysun.com/opinion/why-i-let-my-9-year-old-ride-subway-alone/73976. For a similar perspective, see Kim Brooks, *Small Animals: Parenthood in the Age of Fear* (New York: Flatiron Books, 2018).

5. The free-range kids website and conversation has been rebranded as Let Grow, a 501(c)(3), https://letgrow.org.

6. Susan T. Lennon, "That Little Freckle Could Be a Time Bomb," *Newsweek*, May 23, 2004, https://www.newsweek.com/little-freckle-could-be-time-bomb-128009.

7. WYOU-TV 22, local CBS affiliate news, November 2, 2003, 11:00 edition.

8. Frank Furedi, *Culture of Fear*, rev. ed. (New York: Continuum, 2002), 6.

9. Centers for Disease Control and Prevention, "Leading Causes of Death," CDC, page last reviewed March 17, 2017, https://www.cdc.gov/nchs/fastats/leading-causes-of-death.htm.

10. See Furedi, *Culture of Fear*, 15–44.

11. In data from thirty-five countries that belong to the Organisation for Economic Co-operation and Development, life expectancy increased in every country by more than ten years between 1980 and 2015. National Center for Health Statistics, *Health, United States, 2017*, CDC, accessed October 11, 2019, table 14, https://www.cdc.gov/nchs/data/hus/hus17.pdf.

12. Barry Glassner, *The Culture of Fear* (New York: Basic Books, 1999), 75.

13. The one outlier year was 2001, in which 41 percent of respondents said there was more crime and 43 percent said less. John Gramlich, "5 Facts about Crime in the US," Pew Research Center FactTank, October 17, 2019, https://www.pewresearch.org/fact-tank/2019/10/17/facts-about-crime-in-the-u-s; Gramlich, "Voters' Perceptions of Crime Continue to Conflict with Reality," Pew Research Center FactTank, November 16, 2016, https://www.pewresearch.org/fact-tank/2016/11/16/voters-perceptions-of-crime-continue-to-conflict-with-reality.

14. George Gerbner, "Reclaiming Our Cultural Mythology," *In Context*, no. 38 (Spring 1994), https://www.context.org/iclib/ic38/gerbner. More recently, the Annenberg School ran a study to test the ongoing validity of the "mean world" hypothesis. The study reaffirmed Gerbner's findings "that the American public's fear of crime is statistically related to the amount of violence portrayed on prime-time TV." "Fear of Crime Is Related to the Amount of Violence on Prime-Time Television," Annenberg Public Policy Center, June 18, 2014, https://cdn.annenbergpublicpolicycenter.org/wp-content/uploads/2018/03/TV-violence-fear-of-crime-06-18-14.pdf.

15. Glassner, *Culture of Fear*, xxii, from a Barbara Walters story on *20/20* in 1998.

16. Glassner, *Culture of Fear*, xxii.

17. See Al Franken, *Lies and the Lying Liars Who Tell Them* (New York: Dutton, 2003), 1.

18. From an NPR interview with Joseph Angotti, former senior vice president of NBC News, in Rick Karr, "Moore Film Targets Gun Violence, American Media," *All Things Considered*, November 2, 2002, http://www.npr.org/templates/story/story.php?storyId=829697.

19. Karr, "Moore Film Targets Gun Violence."

20. Joseph Angotti, quoted in Karr, "Moore Film Targets Gun Violence."

21. Associated Press, "Gravely Ill, Atwater Offers Apology," *New York Times*, January 13, 1991, https://www.nytimes.com/1991/01/13/us/gravely-ill-atwater-offers-apology.html.

22. Glassner, *Culture of Fear*, 45–46.

23. See, for instance, the account in Ron Suskind, *The One Percent Doctrine* (New York: Simon and Schuster, 2006), 24–26, 64.

24. George W. Bush, "State of the Union," January 28, 2003, https://georgewbush-whitehouse.archives.gov/news/releases/2003/01/20030128-19.html; Christopher Marquis, "The Struggle for Iraq: Diplomacy; Powell Admits No Hard Proof in Linking Iraq to Al Qaeda," *New York Times*, January 9, 2004, https://www.nytimes.com/2004/01/09/world/struggle-for-iraq-diplomacy-powell-admits-no-hard-proof-linking-iraq-al-qaeda.html.

25. See Colin Powell's admission in Marquis, "Struggle for Iraq."

26. Bill Clinton, "2004 Democratic National Convention Address," July 26, 2004, Boston, http://www.americanrhetoric.com/speeches/convention2004/billclinton2004dnc.htm.

27. Ian Schwartz, "Trump: Mexico Not Sending Us Their Best; Criminals, Drug Dealers and Rapists Are Crossing Border," *Real Clear Politics*, June 16, 2015, https://www.realclearpolitics.com/video/2015/06/16/trump_mexico_not_sending_us_their_best_criminals_drug_dealers_and_rapists_are_crossing_border.html.

28. Anna Flagg, "The Myth of the Criminal Immigrant," *New York Times*, March 30, 2018, https://www.nytimes.com/interactive/2018/03/30/upshot/crime-immigration-myth.html.

29. Kashmira Gander, "Donald Trump's Wind Power Comments Amount to 'Malicious Ignorance,' Scientist Says," *Newsweek*, March 29, 2019, https://www.newsweek.com/donald-trump-wind-power-malicious-ignorance-mocked-1379821.

30. Bishop Paul V. Marshall, "Does God Want Us to Hate Anyone on His Behalf?," *Morning Call*, October 4, 2003, https://www.mcall.com/news/mc-xpm-2003-10-04-3513170-story.html.

31. https://www.feargod.com/fear-god-shirts.html, accessed October 12, 2019.

32. Spencer Burke, *Making Sense of Church* (Grand Rapids: Zondervan, 2003), 129.

33. See John Fischer's discussion of this in *Fearless Faith* (Eugene, OR: Harvest House, 2002).

34. Barbara Brown Taylor, "Fear and the American Church," Columbia Theological Seminary, 2006, accessed October 5, 2019, https://www.ctsnet.edu/at-this-point/fear-american-church.

35. Hans Urs von Balthasar, *The Christian and Anxiety*, trans. Dennis D. Martin and Michael J. Miller (San Francisco: Ignatius Press, 2000), 35.

36. Richard B. Hays, *The Moral Vision of the New Testament* (New York: HarperCollins, 1996), 197.

## Chapter 2: Fear and the Moral Life

1. Simon Harak, *Virtuous Passions* (Mahwah, NJ: Paulist Press, 1993), 2.
2. Harak, *Virtuous Passions*, 22–22.
3. Andreas Olsson and Elizabeth A. Phelps, "Social Learning of Fear," *Nature Neuroscience* 10, no. 9 (2007): 1095–102.
4. Walter Brueggemann, "The Liturgy of Abundance, the Myth of Scarcity," *Christian Century*, March 24–31, 1999, https://www.religion-online.org /article/the-liturgy-of-abundance-the-myth-of-scarcity.
5. H. Richard Niebuhr, *The Responsible Self* (San Francisco: HarperSanFrancisco, 1963), 60.
6. Niebuhr, *The Responsible Self*, 140.
7. Joseph LeDoux, "'Run, Hide, Fight' Is Not How Our Brains Work," *New York Times*, December 18, 2015, https://www.nytimes.com/2015/12/20 /opinion/sunday/run-hide-fight-is-not-how-our-brains-work.html.
8. Thomas Aquinas, *Summa Theologiae* I-II, q. 44, art. 1, trans. Fathers of the English Dominican Province (Allen, TX: Christian Classics, 1948).
9. See Aquinas, *Summa Theologiae* I-II, q. 65, art. 5; Westminster Shorter Catechism, q. 1.
10. Frank Furedi, *Culture of Fear*, rev. ed. (New York: Continuum, 2002), 147.
11. Furedi, *Culture of Fear*, 25, citing M. Hillman, J. Adams, and J. Whiteleg, *One False Move . . . A Study of Children's Independent Mobility* (London: PSI Publishing, 1990), 111.
12. Patty Dann, "The End of the Long-Distance Marriage," *New York Times*, April 17, 2020, https://www.nytimes.com/2020/04/17/style/modern -love-coronavirus-end-of-long-distance-marriage.html.
13. George W. Bush, "President Bush Delivers Graduation Speech at West Point," June 1, 2002, https://georgewbush-whitehouse.archives.gov/news/re leases/2002/06/20020601-3.html.
14. The 2014 US Senate Select Committee on Intelligence's report on the CIA detention and interrogation program concluded that "the use of the CIA's enhanced interrogation techniques was not an effective means of obtaining accurate information or gaining detainee cooperation." CNN Library, "CIA Torture Report Fast Facts," September 12, 2019, https://www.cnn.com /2015/01/29/us/cia-torture-report-fast-facts/index.html.
15. Michael Tomasky, "Has Political Fear-Mongering Lost Its Appeal?," *New York Times*, June 18, 2016, https://www.nytimes.com/2016/06/19/opin ion/campaign-stops/has-political-fear-mongering-lost-its-appeal.html.
16. Jeremy Diamond, "Trump: Paris Massacre Would Have Been 'Much Different' If People Had Guns," CNN, November 15, 2014, https://www .cnn.com/2015/11/14/politics/paris-terror-attacks-donald-trump-guns/in dex.html.

17. Dick Cheney, interview by Tim Russert, *Washington Post*, September 16, 2001, https://www.washingtonpost.com/wp-srv/nation/specials/attacked/transcripts/cheney091601.html.

18. Bruce Springsteen, "Devils and Dust," track 1 on *Devils and Dust*, Columbia Records, 2005, compact disc.

19. Jon Ungoed-Thomas and David Leppard, "Shoot to Kill without Warning," *London Times*, July 31, 2005, https://www.thetimes.co.uk/article/shoot-to-kill-without-warning-kh5dgj0b69w.

20. "Slain Brazilian's Family Wants Answers," Al Jazeera, August 6, 2005, https://www.aljazeera.com/archive/2005/08/20084915517855282.html.

## Chapter 3: Why Fearlessness Is a Bad Idea

1. For an account of this story see Jacob and Wilhelm Grimm, "The Story of a Boy Who Went Forth to Learn Fear," trans. D. L. Ashliman, available at http://www.pitt.edu/~dash/grimm004.html.

2. Thomas Aquinas, *Summa Theologiae* II-II, q. 19, art. 3, trans. Fathers of the English Dominican Province (Allen, TX: Christian Classics, 1948).

3. Aquinas, *Summa Theologiae* II-II, q. 126, art. 1.

4. Karl Barth, *Church Dogmatics* III/3, ed. G. W. Bromiley and T. F. Torrance, trans. G. W. Bromiley and R. J. Ehrlich (Edinburgh: T&T Clark, 1960), 295–99.

5. Augustine, *Confessions* 4.4.9, 4.8.13, 4.10.15, trans. Maria Boulding, OSB (New York: Random House, 1997), 59, 62, 63.

6. Cited in Corey Robin, *Fear: The History of a Political Idea* (Oxford: Oxford University Press, 2004), 132.

7. Aquinas, *Summa Theologiae* I-II, q. 44, art. 4.

8. Benedict, *Rule of Benedict*, trans. Leonard J. Doyle, OblSB (Collegeville, MN: Order of Saint Benedict, 2001), chap. 4, no. 47, http://archive.osb.org/rb/text/toc.html.

9. Joseph Cardinal Bernardin, *The Gift of Peace* (New York: Doubleday, 1997), 93.

10. Bernardin, *Gift of Peace*, 109.

11. Howard Thurman, *Jesus and the Disinherited* (Boston: Beacon Press, 1976), 36–38.

12. Yonat Shimron, "Study Links Anti-Muslim Discrimination with Radicalization," Religion News Service, July 10, 2018, https://religionnews.com/2018/07/10/internet-search-study-finds-link-between-muslim-hate-and-radicalization.

13. Shimron, "Study Links Anti-Muslim Discrimination with Radicalization."

14. Ellen F. Davis, *Getting Involved with God: Rediscovering the Old Testament* (Cambridge, MA: Cowley Publications, 2001), 102.

15. Davis, *Getting Involved with God*, 102–3.

16. Davis, *Getting Involved with God*, 103.

17. Shmuley Boteach, *Face Your Fear* (New York: St. Martin's Press, 2004), 8.

18. Aquinas, *Summa Theologiae* II-II, q. 126, art. 1.

19. George W. Bush, "State of the Union Address," February 2, 2005, https://georgewbush-whitehouse.archives.gov/news/releases/2005/02/2005 0202-11.html.

20. C. S. Lewis, *The Four Loves* (New York: Harcourt, Brace and Company, 1960), 168.

21. Lewis, *Four Loves*, 169.

## Chapter 4: Putting Fear in Its Place

1. I am aware that the left-brain, right-brain distinction is heuristic and does not rely on a discrete left and right location for particular brain functions. But the distinction does help us name the various ways our mind can work on a problem. For a fascinating exploration, see Ian McGilchrist, *The Master and His Emissary: The Divided Brain and the Making of the Western World*, 2nd ed. (New Haven: Yale University Press, 2019).

2. Thomas Aquinas, *Summa Theologiae* I-II, q. 42, art. 3, trans. Fathers of the English Dominican Province (Allen, TX: Christian Classics, 1948).

3. Following Aristotle, who said, "Of the faults that are committed one consists in fearing what one should not, another in fearing as we should not, another in fearing when we should not, and so on." Aristotle, *Nicomachean Ethics* 3.7, accessed February 2, 2004, http://classics.mit.edu/Aristotle/nico machaen.3.iii.html.

4. Aquinas, *Summa Theologiae* I-II, q. 42, art. 2.

5. George Gerbner, "Reclaiming Our Cultural Mythology," *In Context*, no. 38 (Spring 1994), https://www.context.org/iclib/ic38/gerbner.

6. Aquinas, *Summa Theologiae* II-II, q. 19, art. 3.

7. Aquinas, *Summa Theologiae* II-II, q. 125, art. 2.

8. Aquinas, *Summa Theologiae* II-II, q. 125, art. 1.

9. Aquinas, *Summa Theologiae* I-II, q. 43, art. 2.

10. Aquinas, *Summa Theologiae* II-II, q. 125, art. 4.

11. As Aquinas puts it, joy "is caused by love, either through the presence of the thing loved, or because the proper good of the thing loved exists and endures in it; and the latter is the case chiefly in the love of benevolence, whereby a man rejoices in the well-being of his friend, though he be absent." Aquinas, *Summa Theologiae* II-II, q. 28, art. 1.

12. Hans Urs von Balthasar, *The Christian and Anxiety*, trans. Dennis D. Martin and Michael J. Miller (San Francisco: Ignatius Press, 2000), 88.

13. Dietrich Bonhoeffer, *The Cost of Discipleship* (New York: Macmillan, 1959), 99.

14. David Ford, *The Shape of Living* (Grand Rapids: Baker, 1997).

15. Ford, *Shape of Living*, 17.

16. Ford, *Shape of Living*, 66.

17. James Finley, "Freedom from Fear," Center for Action and Contemplation, October 25, 2018, https://cac.org/freedom-from-fear-2018-10-25.

18. Richard Rohr, *Everything Belongs* (New York: Crossroad, 2003), 143.

### Chapter 5: Community and Courage

1. Frank Furedi, *Culture of Fear*, rev. ed. (New York: Continuum, 2002), 67–68.

2. Furedi, *Culture of Fear*, 172.

3. "A Lifelong Commitment," Taizé, last updated November 20, 2010, http://www.taize.fr/en_article6.html.

4. Otto Selles, "Taizé in the Fall: A Parable of Community," *Books & Culture*, November 29, 2005, https://www.booksandculture.com/articles/web exclusives/2005/november/051128.html.

5. Aquinas, *Summa Theologiae* II-II, q. 123, art. 6, trans. Fathers of the English Dominican Province (Allen, TX: Christian Classics, 1948).

6. Hans Urs von Balthasar, *The Christian and Anxiety*, trans. Dennis D. Martin and Michael J. Miller (San Francisco: Ignatius Press, 2000), 152–53.

7. Aristotle, *Nicomachean Ethics* 3.7, trans. W. D. Ross, in Richard McKeon, ed., *Introduction to Aristotle* (New York: Random House, 1947), 363.

8. Paul J. Wadell, *Friendship and the Moral Life* (Notre Dame, IN: University of Notre Dame Press, 1989), xiii.

9. John Milbank, *Theology and Social Theory: Beyond Secular Reason* (Oxford: Basil Blackwell, 1990), 411.

10. See Claude Payne and Hamilton Beazley, *Reclaiming the Great Commission* (New York: Jossey-Bass, 2000).

11. Yann Martel, *Life of Pi* (Orlando, FL: Harcourt, 2001), 161.

12. Martel, *Life of Pi*, 161–62.

13. Toni Morrison, "Nobel Lecture," Nobel Prize website, December 7, 1993, https://www.nobelprize.org/prizes/literature/1993/morrison/lecture.

14. Morrison, "Nobel Lecture."

15. Wadell, *Friendship and the Moral Life*, 164.

### Chapter 6: Trust and Hope

1. R. Kendall Soulen, *The God of Israel and Christian Theology* (Minneapolis: Fortress, 1996), 115.

2. Soulen, *God of Israel and Christian Theology*, 115–17.

3. Simone Weil, *Waiting for God*, trans. Emma Craufurd (New York: Harper and Row, 1951), 166.

4. Martha C. Nussbaum, *The Monarchy of Fear: A Philosopher Looks at Our Political Crisis* (New York: Simon & Schuster, 2019), 243.

5. Barbara Brown Taylor, "Fear and the American Church," Columbia Theological Seminary, 2006, accessed October 5, 2019, https://www.ctsnet.edu/at-this-point/fear-american-church.

6. Taylor, "Fear and the American Church."

7. Taylor, "Fear and the American Church."

8. Nussbaum, *Monarchy of Fear*, 206.

9. Nussbaum, *Monarchy of Fear*, 206.

10. The People's Supper, accessed November 3, 2019, https://thepeoples supper.org.

11. Krista Tippett, "Jennifer Bailey and Lennon Flowers: An Invitation to Brave Space," *On Being* (podcast), October 17, 2019, https://onbeing.org /programs/jennifer-bailey-and-lennon-flowers-an-invitation-to-brave-space.

12. Tippett, "Jennifer Bailey and Lennon Flowers."

13. Rowan Williams, "Archbishop's Easter Day Sermon 2005," Canterbury Cathedral, March 27, 2005, http://aoc2013.brix.fatbeehive.com/articles.php /1616/archbishops-easter-day-sermon-2005.

14. Williams, "Archbishop's Easter Day Sermon."

## Chapter 7: Narrative and Providence

1. John Calvin, *Institutes of the Christian Religion* 1.17.10, ed. John T. McNeill, trans. Ford Lewis Battles (Philadelphia: Westminster Press, 1960), 223.

2. Calvin, *Institutes of the Christian Religion* 1.17.11 (trans. Battles, 224).

3. The following paragraphs draw on Langdon Gilkey's helpful analysis of the demise of providence in modernity. Gilkey, "The Concept of Providence in Contemporary Theology," *Journal of Religion* 43, no. 3 (July 1963): 171–92.

4. Bent Mohn, "Talk with Isak Dinesen," *New York Times*, November 3, 1957, https://www.nytimes.com/1957/11/03/archives/talk-with-isak-dinesen .html, quoted in Barbara Brown Taylor, *God in Pain* (Nashville: Abingdon, 1998), 106.

5. Taylor, *God in Pain*, 106–7.

6. Erich Auerbach, *Mimesis: The Representation of Reality in Western Literature*, trans. Willard R. Trask (Princeton: Princeton University Press, 1953), 73–74.

7. Auerbach, *Mimesis*, 74.

8. For such a reading of Jewish history as well as a helpful discussion of the role of the "master story" in religious traditions, see Michael Goldberg, *Why Should Jews Survive?* (New York: Oxford University Press, 1995).

9. Hans Frei, *The Identity of Jesus Christ* (Philadelphia: Fortress, 1975), 161.

10. Elie Wiesel, *Night* (New York: Bantam Books, 1982), 42.

11. Samuel Wells, *Improvisation: The Drama of Christian Ethics* (Grand Rapids: Brazos, 2004).

12. Wells, *Improvisation*, 57.

13. Flannery O'Connor, *The Habit of Being* (New York: Farrar, Straus and Giroux, 1988), 57.

## Chapter 8: Security and Vulnerability

1. David Daily, personal correspondence, April 14, 1999.
2. Augustine, *Confessions* 4.16.31, trans. Maria Boulding, OSB (New York: Random House, 1997), 73–74.
3. Craig Whitlock, "At Auschwitz, Pope Invokes a 'Heartfelt Cry,'" *Washington Post*, May 29, 2006, http://www.washingtonpost.com/wp-dyn/con tent/article/2006/05/28/AR2006052800453.html.
4. For what follows see Samuel Wells, *Improvisation: The Drama of Christian Ethics* (Grand Rapids: Brazos, 2004), 103–42.
5. Wells, *Improvisation*, 134.
6. Wells provides an interesting discussion of "reincorporation" in *Improvisation*, 143–53.
7. Wells, *Improvisation*, 110.

## Chapter 9: The Risk of Hospitality

1. C. S. Lewis, *The Lion, the Witch and the Wardrobe* (New York: Macmillan, 1950), 75–76.
2. Marc Schultz, "Dangerous Reading," *Creative Loafing*, July 17, 2003, https://www.cltampa.com/home/article/20714638/dangerous-reading.
3. Peter Baker and Michael D. Shear, "El Paso Shooting Suspect's Manifesto Echoes Trump's Language," *New York Times*, August 4, 2019, https://www.nytimes.com/2019/08/04/us/politics/trump-mass-shootings.html.
4. Simon Romero, Caitlin Dickerson, Miriam Jordan, and Patricia Mazzei, "'It Feels like Being Hunted': Latinos across U.S. in Fear after El Paso Massacre," *New York Times*, August 6, 2019, https://www.nytimes.com/2019/08 /06/us/el-paso-shooting-latino-anxiety.html.
5. Lorne Matalon, "Extending 'Zero Tolerance' to People Who Help Migrants along the Border," National Public Radio, May 28, 2019, https://www .npr.org/2019/05/28/725716169/extending-zero-tolerance-to-people-who -help-migrants-along-the-border.
6. Zygmunt Bauman, *Community: Seeking Safety in an Insecure World* (Malden, MA: Polity, 2001), 1–2.
7. Bauman, *Community*, 2.
8. Bauman, *Community*, 145.
9. Philip D. Kenneson and James L. Street, *Selling Out the Church: The Dangers of Church Marketing* (Nashville: Abingdon, 1997), 88–106.
10. Brian McLaren, *More Ready Than You Realize* (Grand Rapids: Zondervan, 2002), 137–40.
11. Christine D. Pohl, *Making Room: Recovering Hospitality as a Christian Tradition* (Grand Rapids: Eerdmans, 1999), 141.
12. Pohl, *Making Room*, 136.
13. Adalbert de Vogüé, *The Rule of Saint Benedict: A Doctrinal and Spiritual Commentary*, trans. J. B. Hasbrouck (Kalamazoo, MI: Cistercian Publications, 1983), 261–62, cited in Pohl, *Making Room*, 139.

14. Louis J. Barletta, mayor of Hazleton, Pennsylvania, had just endorsed an ordinance that fined landlords $1,000 per day for renting to illegal immigrants, banned businesses that hire illegal immigrants from doing business with the city, and made English the official language of the city. Mayor Barletta was quoted as saying, "They don't belong here. They're not legal citizens and I don't want them here." Dan Harris, "Man on a Mission," *Guilt or Innocence?*, aired June 22, 2006, on ABC News.

15. Andrew Gerns, rector, Trinity Episcopal Church, Easton, PA, personal correspondence, used by permission.

## Chapter 10: The Risk of Peacemaking

1. Mary Pope Osborne, *Summer of the Sea Serpent* (New York: Random House, 2004), 81–86.

2. "NCC Releases Ecumenical Pastoral Letter on Iraq," National Council of Churches, May 11, 2004, http://www.ncccusa.org/news/04iraqpastoral letter.html.

3. Benedictine Monks of the Weston Priory, "Statement from Benedictine Men & Women on the Preparations for War," October 12, 2002, http://www .westonpriory.org/iraq.html.

4. Douglas John Hall, "The Mystery of God's Dominion," in *God and the Nations* (Minneapolis: Fortress, 1995), 23.

5. John L. O'Sullivan, *New York Morning News*, December 27, 1845, cited in Walter A. McDougall, *Promised Land, Crusader State: The American Encounter with the World since 1776* (New York: Houghton Mifflin, 1997), 84.

6. William E. Channing to Henry Clay, 1837, quoted in John M. Blum et al., *The National Experience: A History of the United States*, 6th ed. (New York: Harcourt Brace Jovanovich, 1985), 276, cited in Michael T. Lubragge, "Manifest Destiny: The Philosophy That Created a Nation," American History, accessed October 18, 2019, http://www.let.rug.nl/usa/essays/1801-1900 /manifest-destiny/manifest-destiny---the-philosophy-that-created-a-nation .php.

7. Senator Albert J. Beveridge, "In Support of an American Empire," US Senate, Washington, DC, January 9, 1900, *Record*, 56 Cong., I Sess., 704–12, available at http://www.mtholyoke.edu/acad/intrel/ajb72.htm.

8. Beveridge, "In Support of an American Empire."

9. Senator Albert J. Beveridge, "The March of the Flag," campaign speech, September 16, 1898, in *Modern History Sourcebook*, last revised January 21, 2020, http://www.fordham.edu/halsall/mod/1898beveridge.html.

10. George W. Bush, "State of the Union Address," January 20, 2004, https://georgewbush-whitehouse.archives.gov/news/releases/2004/01/2004 0120-7.html.

11. Donald Trump, "Inaugural Address," January 20, 2017, https://www .bartleby.com/124/pres70.html.

12. Jason Le Miere, "Scott Pruitt Told Donald Trump He Is President Because of 'God's Providence' in Resignation Letter," *Newsweek*, July 5, 2018, https://www.newsweek.com/scott-pruitt-donald-trump-god-1010529.

13. Mike Pence, interview by David Brody, Christian Broadcasting Network, 2016, https://www1.cbn.com/content/brody-file-exclusive-mike-pence-talks-about-divine-providence-and-donald-trump.

14. William R. Hutchison and Hartmut Lehmann, eds., *Many Are Chosen: Divine Election and Western Nationalism*, Harvard Theological Studies 38 (Minneapolis: Fortress, 1994).

15. T. S. Eliot, *Murder in the Cathedral* (New York: Harcourt Brace Jovanovich, 1935), 73.

16. Eliot, *Murder in the Cathedral*, 69.

17. Eliot, *Murder in the Cathedral*, 70.

18. T. S. Eliot, *Four Quartets* (New York: Harcourt Brace Jovanovich, 1943), 56, 57, 59.

19. Daniel M. Bell Jr., *Just War as Christian Discipleship*, Ekklesia Project, pamphlet 14 (Eugene, OR: Wipf and Stock, 2005), 11, http://d1swb5 ay1qopx0.cloudfront.net/wp-content/uploads/2016/07/EP-pamphlet-14.pdf.

20. Bell, "Just War as Christian Discipleship," 20.

21. Jérôme Bindé, "Toward an Ethics of the Future," *Public Culture* 12, no. 1 (2000): 52.

22. Bell, "Just War as Christian Discipleship," 20.

23. "Statement by Alabama Clergymen," April 12, 1963, Martin Luther King, Jr., Research and Education Institute, Stanford University, https://king institute.stanford.edu/sites/mlk/files/lesson-activities/clergybirmingham1 963.pdf.

24. Martin Luther King Jr., "Letter from a Birmingham Jail," April 16, 1963, Center for Africana Studies, University of Pennsylvania, https://www .africa.upenn.edu/Articles_Gen/Letter_Birmingham.html.

25. Martin Luther King Jr., "'I Have a Dream,' Address Delivered at the March on Washington for Jobs and Freedom" (speech, Washington, DC, August 28, 1963), Martin Luther King, Jr., Research and Education Institute, Stanford University, https://kinginstitute.stanford.edu/king-papers/documents /i-have-dream-address-delivered-march-washington-jobs-and-freedom.

26. King, "I Have a Dream."

27. Martin Luther King Jr., "Where Do We Go from Here?" (speech, Atlanta, GA, August 16, 1967), Martin Luther King, Jr., Research and Education Institute, Stanford University, https://kinginstitute.stanford.edu/king -papers/documents/where-do-we-go-here-address-delivered-eleventh-annu al-sclc-convention.

## Chapter 11: The Risk of Generosity

1. Walter Brueggemann, "Enough Is Enough," John Mark Ministries, January 3, 2003, http://jmm.aaa.net.au/articles/1181.htm.

2. Aquinas, *Summa Theologiae* II-II, q. 125, art. 4, trans. Fathers of the English Dominican Province (Allen, TX: Christian Classics, 1948).

3. Adam Smith, *The Wealth of Nations*, Modern Library ed. (New York: Random House, 1947), 423.

4. Adam Smith, *Theory of Moral Sentiments* 4.1, 6th ed. (London: A. Millar, 1790), Library of Economics and Liberty, accessed February 25, 2020, http://www.econlib.org/library/Smith/smMS.html.

5. Smith, *Theory of Moral Sentiments* 4.1.

6. Smith, *Theory of Moral Sentiments* 4.1.

7. Smith, *Theory of Moral Sentiments* 4.1.

8. John Milbank, *Theology and Social Theory: Beyond Secular Reason* (Oxford: Basil Blackwell, 1990), 29.

9. Milbank, *Theology and Social Theory*, 29.

10. The following paragraphs draw on Walter Brueggemann, "The Liturgy of Abundance, the Myth of Scarcity," *Christian Century*, March 24–31, 1999, Religion Online, https://www.religion-online.org/article/the-liturgy-of-abundance-the-myth-of-scarcity.

11. Brueggemann, "Liturgy of Abundance."

12. Brueggemann, "Liturgy of Abundance."

13. Christopher Franks, "Thomas's Economics and the Redundancy of Natural Law" (paper presented at the Society of Christian Ethics Annual Meeting, Chicago, IL, January 11, 2004).

14. John Calvin, *Institutes of the Christian Religion* 3.7.5, ed. John T. McNeill, trans. Ford Lewis Battles (Philadelphia: Westminster Press, 1960), 695.

15. Aquinas, *Summa Theologiae* II-II, q. 66, art. 2, trans. Fathers of the English Dominican Province (Allen, TX: Christian Classics, 1948).

16. Calvin, *Institutes of the Christian Religion* 3.7.8 (trans. Battles, 698).

17. This reading comes from a sermon preached by Bob Dunham at University Presbyterian Church, Chapel Hill, NC.

18. Pura Vida Coffee, "Our Mission," accessed April 19, 2020, https://www.puravidacreategood.com/our-mission; for Economy of Communion, a network of businesses embracing Catholic Social Teaching, see https://eocnoam.org/what-is-the-eoc, accessed April 19, 2020.

19. See Luigino Bruni and Stefano Zamagni, *Civil Economy: Efficiency, Equity, Public Happiness* (Bern: Peter Lang, 2007), 181–95. For more on benefit corporations, see B Lab, www.bcorporation.net.

20. Josu Ugarte, quoted in Mary Hansen, "What's Next for the World's Largest Federation of Worker-Owned Co-Ops?," *Yes! Magazine*, June 12, 2015, www.yesmagazine.org/new-economy/world-s-largest-federation-of-worker-owned-co-operatives-mondragon-josu-ugarte.

21. Nate Kaiser, "nPost.com Interview with Craig Newmark," nPost.com, February 25, 2004, http://www.craigslist.org/about/press/npostinterview.html.

22. Matt Richtel, "Craig's To-Do List: Leave Millions on the Table," *New York Times*, September 6, 2004.

23. Ryan Mac, "Craig Newmark Founded Craigslist to Give Back, Now He's a Billionaire," *Forbes*, May 3, 2017, https://www.forbes.com/sites/ryan mac/2017/05/03/how-does-craigslist-make-money/#65fd2e3c27b1.

24. Craigslist, "Mission and History," accessed December 19, 2019, https://www.craigslist.org/about/mission_and_history.

25. Chris Taylor, "A Craigslist Guide to Knowing When You Have Enough to Give Away," Reuters, June 26, 2018, https://www.reuters.com/article/us-money-lifelessons-newmark/a-craigslist-guide-to-knowing-when-you-have-enough-to-give-away-idUSKBN1JM18N.

26. Adam Higginbotham, "Citizen Craig," *Guardian*, August 18, 2006, https://www.theguardian.com/theguardian/2006/aug/18/guardianweekly.guardianweekly11#.

27. Brueggemann, "Enough Is Enough."

# ABOUT THE AUTHOR

**Scott Bader-Saye** (PhD, Duke University) is the academic dean and Helen and Everett H. Jones Chair in Christian Ethics and Moral Theology at Seminary of the Southwest in Austin, Texas. His most recent book is *Formed by Love,* a contribution to the series Church's Teaching for a Changing World. He is also the author of *Church and Israel after Christendom: The Politics of Election* and has contributed to *The Blackwell Companion to Christian Ethics* (2nd ed., 2011) and *The Cambridge Companion to the Gospels* (2nd ed., 2020). He has published widely in theological journals and magazines.